MW01101112

LEADERSHIP AND ADMINISTRATION OF SUCCESSFUL ARCHIVAL PROGRAMS

Leadership and Administration of Successful Archival Programs

EDITED BY

Bruce W. Dearstyne

THE GREENWOOD LIBRARY MANAGEMENT COLLECTION

Gerard B. McCabe, Series Adviser

Greenwood Press
WESTPORT, CONNECTICUT • LONDON

Library of Congress Cataloging-in-Publication Data

Leadership and administration of successful archival programs / edited by Bruce W. Dearstyne.
    p. cm.—(Greenwood library management collection, ISSN 0894–2986)
   ISBN 0–313–31575–2 (alk. paper)
   1. Archives—Administration. 2. Leadership. I. Dearstyne, Bruce W. (Bruce William), 1944– II. Series.
  CD950.L43 2001
  025.1'97—dc21   2001033732

British Library Cataloguing in Publication Data is available.

Library of Congress Catalog Card Number: 2001033732
ISBN: 0–313–31575–2
ISSN: 0894–2986

First published in 2001

Greenwood Press, 88 Post Road West, Westport, CT 06881
An imprint of Greenwood Publishing Group, Inc.
www.greenwood.com

Printed in the United States of America

The paper used in this book complies with the Permanent Paper Standard issued by the National Information Standards Organization (Z39.48–1984).

10 9 8 7 6 5 4 3 2 1

Contents

Introduction

This is a book about program building—leadership, planning, administration, and strategic approaches used by dynamic, successful archival programs. Through a series of essays by people marked by excellence in program administration and professional attainment, the book explores what it takes to overcome the challenges of limited resources, changing user expectations, changing formats, and other factors, and to make archival programs succeed. The archival literature has little coverage of leadership issues; this book is intended to provide guidance on exemplary practices and programs.

The articles provide varying perspectives, insights, advice, caveats, and other helpful information based on the experiences of people who have actually developed and administered successful programs.

Richard Cox discusses the role of archival education in preparing leaders of archival programs. Frank Burke's article explores several themes of supervision and leadership. Larry Hackman explores the factors that account for strong, successful programs. Liisa Fagerlund brings an international perspective and shows the need to tailor leadership style to fit institutional realities. Michael Kurtz explores strategic planning at the National Archives and Records Administration. Phil Mooney explains what is required to operate a business archives successfully. Lauren Brown discusses administrative approaches that are needed for a university archives/manuscripts program. My first article attempts to summarize the traits of successful programs and to analyze leadership skills. My concluding article in the book offers additional insights and documents that illustrate successful, innovative approaches to building strong programs.

Several themes come through in the chapters in the book. The leadership role of the program director is critical in shaping the program and determining its direction and success. The authors exemplify varying leadership styles, but each one was appropriate for the setting and the times where he or she operated. The authors make clear that considerable energy and commitment are required for successful program leadership. Programs need to be customized to fit their settings and to reinforce the objectives of their parent institutions. Successful programs seem to keep on the move, growing and expanding as needs change and opportunities emerge. The essays show the need to balance consistency and continuity with adaptiveness and versatility. Program building and development seems to require, or call forth, a different set of skills than administration or management of a program that is relatively placid and not changing. Education plays an important role in the preparation of archival leadership. The skills and approaches reflected in the essays are similar in many ways to those needed for successful leadership in other settings such as business and government.

I am grateful to the authors of these chapters for sharing their insights and perspectives.

I am also very grateful to Jane Garry, our editor at Greenwood Press, for her advice and guidance as the book was under development.

Finally, I want to thank my wife, Susan, for working with me in editing the manuscript and for indexing the book. For nearly thirty years, Susan has been my partner in research and writing, and I am very grateful for her patience, support, and work.

Bruce W. Dearstyne
College Park, Maryland

1

Leadership and Archival Education

Richard J. Cox

INTRODUCTION

If the quality of leadership in the archival field depends on the availability of individuals who rise to become leaders (which it does), then an important question is—where do these leaders come from? I hold to a simple premise that leaders are made, not born, although giving individuals with leadership qualities the opportunity to develop and use them is the critical matter. Holding to such a belief suggests other questions: How are they made? Do leaders emerge from within the ranks of the field, based on a peculiar mix of education, experiences, and personal traits? Do special challenges create circumstances making new leaders?

This chapter explores one aspect of the making of archival leaders, the relationship of education to leadership. Does the educational background of archivists contribute to their emergence as leaders? What does the obvious recent growth in graduate archival education have to do with the question of leadership within the field? Are archival educational programs, any or all, self-consciously trying to train leaders for the future? These are questions not really considered before because of the previously limited nature of archival education. Now, with a growing corps of full-time, regular faculty teaching archival studies and separate master's degrees and expanded curriculum, such issues are worth considering. The chapter also considers another aspect of archival leadership. What are the leadership responsibilities of this new professional, the archival educator? As is obvious from this chapter, the answers are not yet clear and reflect the fact that our educational programs are still in a transition stage somewhere between apprenticeship and fully developed graduate programs.

ARCHIVAL EDUCATION AND THE PRODUCTION OF LEADERS

If we were writing this book several decades ago, it is doubtful that we might even have considered archival education as a part of leadership. Despite considerable attention by our professional associations to matters like mission and planning, these associations seemed to assume that leaders were available and suggested little of a role for education (except to educate policy makers and the public about the nature and importance of archives, archivists, and archival work). Until the beginning of substantial changes in the educational infrastructure in the mid 1980s, the archival profession focused on short-term training in basic work while its associations stressed long-term planning. Apprenticeships, workshops, institutes, and the traditional three course sequence often taught by adjuncts provided little opportunity to consider matters of leadership or broader professional issues and trends since the focus was on short-term training. The limitations of these earlier educational programs may explain why professional associations like the Society of American Archivists did not naturally think of them as sources for individuals to lead the profession into the future.[1]

This older educational model turned out excellent practitioners, with its bench-like focus on archival work. There is certainly no question that from this approach emerged some future leaders (although they often had to gain the broader perspective needed for leadership by immersion into the field).[2] As far as leadership is concerned, the emphasis then seemed to be on leaders being born, or at least developing from innate traits and other interests and incidents. While certain aspects of the archival field, like bench conservation, require very traditional apprenticeships because of the nature of the work involved, it is obvious that training of this sort is severely handicapped in turning out individuals who would want to assume leadership roles with views much broader than the individual objects they work on in their repositories.[3] This old approach can nurture skills and attitudes, including a substantial socialization to the field. But it is limited, not addressing the needs to contribute to professional knowledge, resolve ever-changing challenges such as those posed by technologies, or prepare practitioners to deal with unanticipated future consequences of changing recordkeeping practices. If a person happens to connect with a dynamic leader, either early in the career or even while they are in the classroom, then such limitations might be counterbalanced.[4]

We have some notable instances of individuals who became leaders in the field being mentored by archival leaders who were also teaching as adjuncts. F. Gerald Ham's teaching at the University of Wisconsin at Madison while State Archivist is one example, at least partly attributable to Ham's interest in change in the profession as exemplified by his writings on appraisal and collecting.[5] We continually run across professional leaders who were mentored by Ham through the courses he taught.[6] This perhaps suggests that the mentoring role, in the old days or the present, is one way in which educators play a role in developing future archival leaders. Individuals in the courses taught by educators are certainly influenced by perspectives presented by these teachers within the classroom (no matter how careful we are in trying to present differing viewpoints and introducing students to the many debates within the field), through closer interaction in research and writing papers for these courses, and in subsequent relationships maintained in the years after graduation. Still, the old "lone arranger" model, with the expectation that most graduates of these old and present programs will go out and work as the solitary professional and do everything, puts pressure on trying to orient students new to the field to all functions and responsibilities.[7] This diverts attention away from examining in the classroom the critical responsibilities of leadership within the field or any expectation that these students when they graduate may assume leadership responsibilities within a particular organization.

Under the old model of archival training, the birthing of leaders would have to be an accidental process, depending on a fortuitous attraction of the right individuals to the profession and to the right part of the discipline whereby these individuals could get to meetings, assume professional positions, develop networks, become known, and demonstrate a capacity for leadership. In other words, except for what might happen between a student with leadership qualities and interests and their teacher, people coming through these earlier education programs just figured out the business of leadership on their own (or they ignored it). The focus of these earlier programs was on basic archival functions, as you would expect from apprenticeship. Could the expansion of graduate archival education, as has occurred in the past two decades, perhaps make the process of identifying and developing professional leaders less of an accidental process? It is worth some consideration.

For the past twenty years we have witnessed the development of multiple course curriculum far exceeding the old three-course model (that was really just two courses and fieldwork) along with the emergence of a substantial regular faculty (including in a small number of places multiple faculty). Slower to develop has been separate master's degree programs, but there is some evidence to suggest that this might be about to change as well.[8] The sheer act of growing such education programs should cause us to reflect on what graduate education supports, what must be taught, and (most importantly for this present chapter) the purpose of what such programs serve. After all, the internal expansion of these programs provides a much greater opportunity for teaching about certain matters than just a few courses would allow. But the expanded programs may have been swallowed up by bigger challenges to deal with, such as technologies (just as the information technology courses pushed out or reformed older emphases such as the history of books and printing) and the preparation of students for the widest range of archival positions (including non-archival positions with the potential for influencing archival work). Moreover, because of the lack of separate degrees, much of the expansion of the program has been directed to building connections with library and information science schools or history departments, and this may have provided a more limited opportunity than what it seems we now have before us.

Some archival educators are recognizing that their graduates may assume non-traditional archival positions but with implications for archival work. Most commonly, graduates may be accepting records management positions. But it is likely we will also see graduates accepting positions with a focus on information resources management, knowledge management, policy, and digital libraries or digital resources management. Archival educators spend an increasing amount of attention weaving these connections, and since some of these areas are relatively new and changing quickly this may challenge educators to put more attention on the use of information technologies and related matters that are vital to these kinds of positions rather than focusing on other topics like management or leadership. The expansion of graduate archival education programs may subsume more new materials, approaches, and responsibilities than we really imagined at any point in the past two decades of this educational growth and change.[9]

In this expansion both of graduate archival programs and the breadth of programs and organizations their graduates might work in, there may be some indirect possibilities for dealing with leadership. In order to demonstrate that archives and archivists are relevant to other fields relating to information and evidence, they will need to describe the value of records and the value of archivists in a manner in which this might be more easily understood by others. Archival educators, in addition to introducing students to the basic knowledge and practices of the field, also take on a heavy responsibility for teaching about advocacy.[10] At the least, given that there is some backlash within the field and within the public sphere over traditional curatorial and cultural roles and their loss, the archival educator will find him or herself considering the matter of how archivists can balance traditional, new, and emerging roles and responsibilities. From my vantage, this means considering some matters of leadership, some of which may be quite new. Whether this can really be taught is, however, another matter both because of the broader pedagogical issues and more mundane matters related to archival education.

Some of the mundane matters can be seen in the inner construction of a single program. When I first arrived at the University of Pittsburgh in 1988 my focus was on course content, the result of having moved from the practitioners' ranks and then needing to turn experience and knowledge into systematic courses. As anyone who has done this knows, making such a move can be both a tedious and time-consuming process. However, the emphasis shifted somewhat from course content as I gained experience in teaching and building a program. This was the result of many factors, including the need to explain what a graduate archival education program included to my non-archivist colleagues and archivists along with the recognition of opportunities to have flexibility within my school for building a graduate program. Building such programs is largely an internal process (although it is one that would be helped by having stronger professional standards and advocates from the outside) of building support, fabricating alliances, and making cogent arguments.[11] In other words, the process of building graduate archival programs is one that is somewhat a leadership process in its own right within a complex and rapidly changing structure of higher education.

While building a program seems to be a process that never ends, doing this leads to a series of questions about what the program represents. For myself, I resolved that my primary purpose is to make my students experts about records and recordkeeping systems, giving them a set of tools for working in a variety of institutional settings, serving diverse constituencies, and facing diverse and continuously more complex records issues ranging from technologies to matters like privacy and access. This did not happen overnight, but it was part of a process of observation about needed changes within the field, a market for our graduates, research about electronic records management, reading, and discussions with an ever-changing group of students. Some within the field criticize such a records centered approach as being more akin to what is represented by a related field—namely records management. In this, I admit that I firmly believe that archives and records management to be inextricably linked (at least in the organizational sense), and this is based on both previous professional experience and my own searching for ways to present the knowledge about archives and records in a logical, coherent fashion. Individual archival educators develop particular frames of reference for teaching, something akin to a leadership role in that faculty lead students (although I prefer to present conflicting viewpoints for students to grapple with)[12] through complicated and controversial issues, case studies, and other concerns stemming from a field that must have a fluid approach to new technologies creating and sustaining records.

Focusing on making these students experts leads to another series of questions. Am I merely equipping these individuals to assume entry-level positions or preparing them to do something else? The impetus for such questions was mostly due to the fact that my emphasis on records and recordkeeping systems was not necessarily the normal or traditional manner in which archivists viewed themselves. Many archivists stress the cultural value of archives, which is quite important (and, I might add of great interest to me), but it is problematic whether this cultural value has been stressed in quite the coherent fashion it needs to function in the modern digital era. The self-image and public profile of archivists remain confused.[13] These images range from historians working as archivists to serve other historians to much broader roles of protecting records for evidence and accountability purposes. In between these two very different perspectives, we find archivists who view themselves as custodians, curators, technicians, policy makers, and in other ways. Is one more appropriate than another? Do they change from institutional setting to another? Grappling with these different roles also relates to another leadership issue, one encompassing focusing on complex and sometimes contradictory professional, personal, and organizational missions. Archival educators, as they teach, discuss the business of making choices, discerning how and when to present one aspect of the mission rather than another.

Trying to situate my program to turn out records experts was another way of equipping individuals to become leaders in organizational and professional change. The students do not focus on immutable notions of archival work, but they learn principles and approaches hopefully enabling them to manage records with archival value in systems constantly undergoing transformation. Moreover, the students learn about the necessity of communicating their principles within organizations and society with those who may not understand and may not share the importance of records and archives. Integrating field experiences that students are participating in as part of their graduate program is another means for students to question and probe how archivists should function as leaders within their organizations. Whether I am succeeding or not is a question that becomes very difficult to answer and sits at the heart of a dilemma facing individuals serving as professors in professional schools in universities. Such faculty often have very conflicted roles between serving the traditional role of scholars, researchers, and educators and having to relate to and serve the interests of a field devoted to often very pragmatic responsibilities.[14]

PERSONAL REFLECTIONS ABOUT CHALLENGES IN LEADERSHIP AND ARCHIVAL EDUCATION

There are many challenges working against weaving leadership within the archives curriculum. Not every student coming into an archives education program wants to be a leader. A study of personality types a few years ago suggests what many of us have long suspected, many are still attracted to the field because they see it as a kind of monastic refuge.[15] My own personal experience in reading letters of reference often suggests this as well, whereby individuals comment on applicants' social dysfunctions, and then indicate that they have the perfect disposition to do the work of an archivist. This is made more difficult by the diversity of students we attract into our educational programs. We have diversity primarily from educational backgrounds and age, and this often suggests an equally disparate set of personal career objectives. Many are still coming into the field because of second or third career choices, and trying to mold such individuals into leaders for the archives field seems to be a tough road to travel. They are often more interested in just making a change, not in changing the profession or public perceptions about it.

Then we have the daunting task of thinking about turning these individuals into professional leaders by inviting them into already crowded one- or two-year programs. Programs are already stretched with courses educating students in basic principles, theory, and methodologies of the archival field, and by our attempts with socializing students to the field by providing them both a historical orientation and assessment of current issues and concerns. Much of the time is already committed to grounding students into archival science, records and recordkeeping systems, and methodologies and practices of the profession. Moreover, many employers want archival education programs to do everything. They want instant, fully equipped experts emanating from the programs. They want new experts on electronic records and automated descriptive standards. The employers often want subject experts, at least for the specialized repositories. They also want managers, often placing even entry-level archivists in reasonably complex positions where they deal with the public and supervise volunteers and technicians. Can we really add leadership as one more objective to this list?

Perhaps the greatest challenge is wrestling with the notion whether leadership can be taught at all. Educator V. A. Howard notes, "Leadership, like creativity or human potential, is not a scientific concept. It belongs in ordinary discourse about practical affairs and achievements and failures."[16] Howard acknowledges that we can teach about leaders or the strategies or skills used in certain situations, but he disagrees that it can be taught as a "how-to" or "procedural" subject: "While it cannot be taught directly, it can be learned depending upon the interpretive abilities and practical opportunities of the learner given everything that has been taught."[17] Maybe we should consider more about this basic pedagogical issue before worrying about whether leadership is an essential topic in graduate archival education programs?

ARCHIVAL EDUCATION, HIGHER EDUCATION, AND LEADERSHIP STUDIES

How does the current state of higher education and its interest in "leadership studies" relate to the role of archival education programs and our broader question of the relationship of education to leadership? All over higher education, courses and programs in "leadership studies" have been established and are being developed, part of what has been termed the "leadership industry," deriving from concern in the corporate world for leadership. Self-help books, seminars, institutes, and college and university leadership programs are all part of this industry.[18] These programs come in all shapes and sizes. In late 1998, it was estimated that there were nearly 700 leadership-development programs at American academic institutions, a doubling from four years before, and a year later the number had risen to 800.[19]

The development of leadership programs in higher education has been meteoric. The first bachelor's degree in leadership only dates to 1992 and is located at the University of Richmond and others offer minors in leadership. One course stresses "ethics, multicultural diversity, communication skills, an understanding of people, and a knowledge of the leadership process," offered in the firm belief that someone with certain attributes can be made a more effective leader by such training.[20] Wright State University offers a two-year program focusing on service and leading by persuasion, not coercion.[21] The Eisenhower Leadership Development Program at Texas A&M University is an interdisciplinary, one-semester course for undergraduates, stressing "classroom instruction, various classroom exercises and activities, and semester-long group projects." The students are exposed to speakers from outside the university representing many leaders in many different fields.[22] Of course, the university's interest in leadership certainly stems from historic notions of what the university's role in society is about. Reed L. Welch writes, "Because every student is a potential leader who can work to create positive change in society, it is not enough to confine education to helping students become more knowledgeable about current issues or about how government works. Education should also encourage the development of skills and attitudes that will result in students being effective leaders in addressing societal and community problems."[23] How far we can stretch this from an archival education perspective is another thing. Certainly the notion of being advocates for the archival mission includes some sense of this if one accepts the notion of records being valuable for society or if one believes in the value of records for accountability, but the leadership notion in higher education is more pervasive than what we archival educators are considering.

The growth in the leadership programs has led many to question their value. One historian notes, "What I'd like to know is how intellectually rigorous it really is. I don't know what leadership studies is. With most academic disciplines, you have some sense of what is being covered, and some sense of the methodologies of instruction." While some note that the graduates of these programs land good positions, a career consultant wonders, "If we're going to have a major in leadership, why not have a major in goodness or wisdom? In some ways, it's subjective, and I'm not sure it can be taught. I'd be looking for practical majors that teach skills—the ability to write and communicate, the ability to reason and research information, the ability to use computers."[24] Another academic, serving on a review panel for funding for a leadership studies program, discerned it to be another example of federal government funding waste and continued: "More important, I was introduced to the leadership-studies cult, a no-less-perfect specimen of late-twentieth-century academic avarice and a precise depth gauge of some recent professorial descents into pap, cant, and jargon." He continues, "In some respects the leadership cult resembles a real culture. It possesses a distinct language. It honors heroes and texts comparatively unknown to the general public. It consistently defines past and present reality on its own terms. And it displays a strong determination to enlarge the spheres of its influence. . . . As leadership scholars snuggle to the new public teat, a new industry and special interest are born."[25] The result of these changes in teaching leadership has been a considerable writing about *what* needs to be taught about leadership, pushing back against those who criticize such programs and who argue that leadership is something that cannot be taught.[26]

Despite all the criticism, some studies examining students within these programs have found many positive results of these programs. Students gained awareness about the "social/civic/political awareness," "increased commitment to service and volunteerism," "improved communication skills," a "higher sense of personal and social responsibility," "increased sense of social/civic/political efficacy," "improved self esteem," "improved problem solving ability," and so forth.[27] None of these attributes would be rejected out of hand by archivists—in fact, many of these kinds of skills and attitudes can be found in archival job advertisements today.

Before the emergence of these leadership studies programs, leadership was thought to be something linked to the particular qualities of certain individuals. Some, in responding to criticisms about these programs, have argued that the new programs provide a more useful concept of leadership because "leadership is a socially constructed reality." According to such a view, "leadership must serve the general needs of society rather than the exclusive needs of corporations or of corporate executives. Post-industrial leadership must be inclusive rather than exclusive; it must focus on the community rather than on the elite. Above all, post-industrial leadership must reject the simplistic, cause–effect, dyadic view of the leadership relationship and replace it with a view that incorporates the complexities of social processes and the pluralistic nature of global society." As a result, "The content of leadership education in the future will cover three broad categories: the evolution of social change and development, the processes that influence social development, and the dynamics of human nature in change processes." Studying and understanding leadership requires examining "emotional arguments and appeal to friendship, language strategies such as metaphors and similes, cultural strategies such as the development of myths, symbols, and rituals, moral strategies that define higher moral ground and the common good, and communication strategies that appeal to common goals among networks of participants."[28] In such sentiments, based on an understanding of human and organizational behavior, we can detect many of the kinds of processes and perspectives that archivists would need in order to be successful in their own repositories.

The kinds of debates along with the kinds of programs in leadership offered suggest some pretty basic approaches archival educators could take with leadership. They could watch for key individuals with special skills, gifts, interests, and try to position them for leadership, perhaps by encouraging these students to nurture these skills through additional education (such as doctoral programs or in programs in other fields like management, business, or the leadership programs). Given the diversity of people at-tracted to graduate archival education programs, it is likely that sooner or later we will have some individuals holding majors or minors in leadership studies in our programs as well, and this may have an impact on how we approach looking at leadership. Leadership also may be a key area for field-work, although fieldwork has been focused on archival processing and ref-erence rather than working areas (such as policy, planning, administration) that might prepare individuals for leadership roles within their organiza-tions and the profession. Perhaps archival educators can redesign the field-work to accommodate leadership issues. Finally, archival educators could direct students with interests in leadership to undertake some study on lead-ership within the archival field, examining both its failure and successes. We have some studies in leadership, but, like so many other areas, these have not been systematic or comprehensive.[29] There are ample materials that could be used by educators in guiding students, from the individual case study drawing on the work of cognitive psychologists to that of political scientists trying to identify all the essential elements of leadership.[30]

What archival educators ought not to do is to try to teach leadership in an already crowded curriculum. Rather, educators should try to build partnerships with other programs that may have leadership as an empha-sis (might as some archival programs tied together history and library and information science programs). Archival educators should refer stu-dents to these opportunities, and they might try to build leadership read-ings from the archival literature and other professional literatures into readings of courses stressing management, public advocacy, access, ap-praisal, and other functions in which leadership is an obvious asset or ne-cessity. Archival educators should recognize the parts of archival education programs that might nurture leadership. As one leadership studies advocate notes, "at the heart of leadership education, most would include the need to train students to grasp the problems and issues facing society, to develop analytical and problem-solving skills, to learn to com-municate and work effectively as members of a team, to have experience working in groups, to learn to work with people of diverse backgrounds, cultures, and academic disciplines, to learn to establish goals and moti-vate others to achieve these goals, and to know to speak and write effec-tively."[31] Most archival educators certainly would not discount such matters, although they might suggest that they are looking (or at least hoping for) to attract students from undergraduate programs who have developed many of these skills.

PARTICULAR AREAS WHERE EDUCATORS MAY SERVE
AS LEADERS

While archival educators might reasonably back away from self-con-
scious teaching about leadership with the expectation of *making* leaders,
there are certain areas where educators themselves have leadership responsibilities. These responsibilities relate to the traditional leadership
roles university faculty play in disciplines. Some of these also have implications for supporting leadership development within the archival field.

One of these areas has been around for twenty years, the responsibility
of archival educators to engage in and support the research, writing, and
publication reflecting about seminal matters, issues, and concerns of the
profession. In the 1980s, some hoped that archivists moving into faculty positions would provide a stimulus for a new research and theoretical literature.[32] In fact, the professional literature has been strengthened in a number
of ways (especially in the proliferation of monographs and volumes of col-
lected essays like the one represented here), although there remain many
gaps in research.[33] This is the primary area where educators serve as leaders within the profession, especially as they can direct masters and doctoral
students into exploring needed areas for research.

This is an area of leadership fraught with problems. The nature of research puts archival educators on a partial collision course with the archives field, as it does between academics and any other profession.
Research brings in a questioning, critical analysis that is often not appreci-
ated by practitioners. This has become especially evident in recent years as
a major emphasis on research about electronic records management has
caused a split between those who advocate evidence and accountability
versus those who hold to a cultural perspective of archives. The arguments
are much more complex than this simple assessment, especially since viewpoints become simplified or compressed in order to present arguments for
supporting one or the other of the perspectives.[34] It is hard to lead when the
profession resists self-reflection, criticism or denies the need for research,
arguing that its chief claim for authority is its ability to be pragmatic and
solve everyday problems with common sense.[35] The resolution to such
problems will come about when new leaders in the archival profession recognize the importance of research as being something of greater applicabil-
ity than merely in the academic realm.

Another leadership responsibility for archival educators is in raising up
future leaders of archival education. At present there is a crisis because of a
shortage of archival educators, as more schools and academic departments
seek to hire regular faculty to teach in archival studies and discover very
small pools of applicants even with a growing number of doctoral students

focused on archival matters. The archival profession still seems to be relying on drawing new faculty from the ranks of experienced practitioners, a shortsighted approach as many of these individuals will have short-lived careers in comparison to professional need (unless we view this merely as plugging the gap). This crisis may seem ironic given the recent growth in the numbers of both educators in regular tenure stream positions and number of doctoral students. This suggests yet another question: Do we have enough time to take advantage of this particular window of opportunity that could lead to stronger archival education programs, the greater availability of these programs across the profession, and the preparation of more researchers and research? No one has any answers to such a question.

Given that archival educators, even when critiquing and calling for change of practice within the profession, must always be partially responsive to the employment needs within the field, leadership by them can only be exercised in research and developing future educators along with nurturing the continued development of their education programs (although some will exercise other leadership roles by holding elected and appointed offices within professional associations). Some might take exception to this, and suggest that archival educators should be leaders in advocating for changes in certain dimensions of archival practice, including working for better legislation, developing stronger professional and technical standards, working with archival programs to generate models of practice, and setting national agendas.[36] Educators can certainly assume roles, but this can never be their priority since they are part of the academic world in which research and teaching are the prime means by which they will gain justification and support for their pioneering efforts. As their programs become established and they gain tenure, these educators might also consider such roles although using their time and talents to become public scholars explaining the nature and importance of archives might be a more worthwhile activity for them and the profession.[37]

It would be easy for educators to sit back and see over a long time how the graduates of their programs move into leadership positions. For masters students this can be directorships and elected and appointed professional positions. For doctoral students this can be through their contributions to research and theory and in the developing of new and improved educational venues. Both require taking a very long view.

But there may be a better way to think of the relationship between archival educators, their programs, and the field. John Nirenberg, an academic focused on leadership, critiques the concept of leadership used in many business schools, where leadership is "thought to mean the act of getting things done with and through people" to one that is evolving to a "covenantal relationship with subordinates." Nirenberg quotes Herman Miller to explain this: "A covenantal relationship rests on a shared commitment to ideas, to issues, to values, to goals, and to management processes. Words such as love, warmth, and personal chemistry are certainly pertinent. Covenantal relationships are open to influence. They fulfill deep needs and enable work to have meaning and to be fulfilling. Covenantal relationships reflect unity, grace, and poise. They are an expression of the sacred nature of relationships."[38] As graduate archival education continues to mature, a covenantal relationship between the education programs and their faculty and the profession is the crucial element needed to these programs to contribute to leadership within the profession.

NOTES

1. A sense of what was happening in this era can be seen in my book, *American Archival Analysis: The Recent Development of the Archival Profession in the United States* (Metuchen, New Jersey: Scarecrow Press, Inc., 1990). While I discuss leadership and education in various parts of this volume, my focus is not as developed as what I am discussing in this essay. In *American Archival Analysis* I stressed professionalism, and this resulted in discussions about education as a means of resolving critical needs in preparing individuals to work as qualified archivists, developing a stronger body of professional knowledge, and in public advocacy about the archival mission. However, except for some concerns about some lack of leadership by professional associations in building stronger educational programs, the matter of education and leadership is not discussed.

2. This is the same dilemma many professions have faced with education and leadership. Harold K. Skramstad, Jr., in considering history museums and directors' posts, considers that the traditional historical training was often a "barrier to effective leadership. Most historians have been trained in the basic issues underlying the pursuit of historical knowledge and in the use of tools of historical research. The objective of the training is to develop a critical and independent mind whose primary loyalty is to a set of professional goals shared among other historians. In approaching the leadership of a historical organization, it is necessary to learn a new set of values and yet not forget the professional preparation that must necessarily provide an intellectual core of values for any director." Harold K. Skramstad, Jr., "The Director's Mask," in *Leadership for the Future: Changing Directorial Roles in American History Museums and Historical Societies*, ed. Bryant F. Tolles, Jr. (Nashville: American Association for State and Local History, 1991), p. 25. In the same volume, see Daniel R. Porter, III, "The Director as Initiator of Professional Standards and Training," pp. 47–62.

3. For an excellent window into the nature of apprenticeship, see Annie Tremmel Wilcox, *A Degree of Mastery: A Journey Through Book Arts Apprenticeship* (New York: Penguin Books, 1999).

4. I was fortunate to have as my advisor Walter Rundell while I was a student at the University of Maryland, completing a masters in history. Rundell was a leader in both the historical and archives disciplines, and he helped me both to

meet other leaders and to see a broader vision for the archives field. His premature death was a loss to many professional groups, but he left an enduring legacy in the individuals he educated and influenced.

5. F. Gerald Ham, "The Archival Edge," *American Archivist* 38 (January 1975): 5–13; "Archival Strategies for the Post-Custodial Era," *American Archivist* 44 (Summer 1981): 207–216; and "Archival Choices: Managing the Historical Record in an Age of Abundance," in *Archival Choices: Managing the Historical Record in an Age of Abundance,* ed. Nancy E. Peace (Lexington: D.C. Heath, 1984), pp. 133–147.

6. As I sat next to Ham at a 1987 conference on education, he leaned over to me and pointed out that four of the five panel members were former students of his. My retort, that at least we knew who to blame for problems in leadership in educational ventures, was intended to be humorous, but it also suggests that even the older model of archival education that was closer to apprenticeship could have an influence on matters like professional leadership.

7. Some of these problems can be seen in the advertisements in entry level professional positions; see my, "Employing Records Professionals in the Information Age," *Information Management Journal* 34 (January 2000): 18–20, 22–23, 26–28, 30, 32–33.

8. A detailed description of this recent growth can be seen in Richard J. Cox, Elizabeth Yakel, David Wallace, Jeannette Bastian, and Jennifer Marshall, "Archival Education in North American Library and Information Science Schools: A Status Report," *Library Quarterly,* forthcoming. A shorter version of this is also scheduled for publication in the *Journal of Education for Library and Information Science.*

9. A good sense of some of the challenges and changes represented by an area like knowledge management can be seen in Bruce W. Dearstyne, "Knowledge Management: Concepts, Strategies, and Prospects," *Records and Information Management Report* 15 (September 1999): 1–14.

10. See my "Advocacy in the Graduate Archives Curriculum: A North American Perspective," *Janus* 1 (1997): 30–41.

11. I have discussed this in my "The Society of American Archivists and Graduate Education: Meeting at the Crossroads," *American Archivist* 63 (Fall/Winter 2000), 368–379.

12. For examples about presenting such conflicting viewpoints, see my "Debating the Future of the Book," *American Libraries* 28 (February 1997): 52–55 and "The Great Newspaper Caper: Backlash in the Digital Age," *First Monday* 5 (December 4, 2000) available at *http://firstmonday.org/issues/issue5_12/cox/.*

13. In February 2001 Charles Schultz shared with the Archives and Archivists Listserv a survey (admittedly unscientific) on the "public persona of the archivist" that raised many of these matters.

14. Derek Bok, *Higher Learning* (Cambridge: Harvard University Press, 1986) provides an excellent orientation to such challenges.

15. Charles R. Schultz, "Personality Types of Archivists," *Provenance* 14 (1996): 15–35.

16. V.A. Howard, "Can Leadership Be Taught?" *Work, Education and Leadership: Essays in the Philosophy of Education,* eds. V.A. Howard and Israel Scheffler (New York: Peter Lang, 1995), p. 104.

17. Howard, "Can Leadership Be Taught?" p. 119.

18. John Huey, "The Leadership Industry," *Fortune*, February 21, 1994: pp. 54–56. From the corporate perspective, see also Glenn Rifkin, "Leadership: Can It Be Learned?" *Forbes* 157 (April 8, 1996): 100ff.

19. William H. Honan, "Programs That Make Leadership Their Goal," *New York Times*, 30 September 1998, C20. For the higher count, see M.K. Schwartz, K. M. Axtman, and F.H. Freeman, *Leadership Education Source Book*, 7th ed. Greensboro, NC: Center for Creative Leadership, 1999.

20. Willis M.Watt, "Leadership for 2001: Teaching Leadership in Communication Behaviors," paper presented at the Annual Meeting of the Central States Communication Association (Oklahoma City, OK, April 7–10, 1994). For a description of the Jepson School of Leadership Studies at the University of Richmond, see Gary Putka, "It's Unlikely Holders of This Sheepskin Will Act Like Sheep—Richmond Leadership School Draws Students Who Long to Rule, Make That Serve," *Wall Street Journal*, 12 November 1992, p. A1.

21. Sue Seitz and Staci Pepitone, "Servant Leadership: A Model for Developing College Students," *Metropolitan Universities: An International Forum* 6 (Summer 1996): 113–122.

22. Reed L. Welch, "Training a New Generation of Leaders," *Journal of Leadership Studies* 7 (Winter 2000): 70–81.

23. Reed L. Welch, "Training a New Generation of Leaders," *Journal of Leadership Studies* 7, no. 1 (2000): 71.

24. Leo Reisberg, "Students gain sense of direction in new field of leadership studies," *The Chronicle of Higher Education* 45 (October 30, 1998): A49–A50.

25. Benjamin DeMott, "Choice Academic Pork: Inside the Leadership-Studies Racket," *Harper's Magazine* 287 (December 1983): 61–67. A response to DeMott notes that it was not hard "to detect a whiff of intellectual snobbery emanating from DeMott and other foes of leadership studies," since "exposing high school and college students around the nation to ideas about leadership, as well as busing them into Washington to visit the State Department, Pentagon, and Congress, is in the best American egalitarian tradition." Jacob Heilbrunn, "Can Leadership Be Studied?" *The Wilson Quarterly* 18 (Spring 1994): 65.

26. See, for example, Gloria Nemerowicz and Eugene Rosi, *Education for Leadership and Social Responsibility* (London: The Falmer Press, 1997).

27. Kathleen Zimmerman-Oster and John C. Burkhardt, "Leadership in the Making: A Comprehensive Examination of the Impact of Leadership Development Programs on Students," *Journal of Leadership Studies* (Summer-Fall 1999): 51–66, see especially pp. 63–64.

28. Joseph C. Rost and Richard A. Barker, "Leadership Education in Colleges: Toward a 21st Century Paradigm," *Journal of Leadership Studies* 7 (Winter 2000): 5, 10.

29. Such as Victor Gondos, Jr., *J. Franklin Jameson and the Birth of the National Archives 1906–1926* (Philadelphia: University of Pennsylvania Press, 1981).

30. See, for example, Howard Garner, in collaboration with Emma Laskin, *Leading Minds: Anatomy of Leadership* (New York: Basic Books, 1995) and James MacGregor Burns, *Leadership* (New York: Harper and Row, 1978).

31. Welch, "Training a New Generation of Leaders," p. 71.

32. Frank G. Burke, "The Future Course of Archival Theory in the United States," *American Archivist* 44 (Winter 1981): 40–46 and Paul Conway, "Archival

Education and the Need for Full-Time Faculty," *American Archivist* 51 (Summer 1988): 254–265.

33. See my "An Analysis of Archival Research, 1970–1992, and the Role and Function of the *American Archivist*," *American Archivist* 57 (Spring 1994): 278–288.

34. For examples of the intensity of feelings about such matters, see Linda Henry, "Schellenberg in Cyberspace," *American Archivist* 16 (Fall 1998): 309–327 and Mark A. Greene, Frank Boles, Richard L. Pifer, Bruce Bruemmer, and Todd J. Daniels-Howell, "The Archivist's New Clothes: or, the Naked Truth about Evidence, Transactions, and Recordness," unpublished paper presented at a seminar at the University of Michigan, January 2001, and made available at *http://www.umich.edu/~iinet/asc/Winter2001/Papers/Greene.pdf*.

35. See the introductory essay in Randall C. Jimerson, ed., *American Archival Studies: Readings in Theory and Practice* (Chicago: Society of American Archivists, 2000).

36. I drew these right from my own much earlier article on a leadership issue, "Leadership and Local Government Records: The Opportunity of the Joint Committee on the Management, Preservation, and Use of Local Government Records," *Midwestern Archivist* 10, no. 1 (1985): 33–41.

37. See my "Accountability, Public Scholarship, and Library, Information, and Archival Science Educators," *Journal of Education for Library and Information Science* 41 (Spring 2000): 94–105.

38. John Nirenberg, "Myths We Teach, Realities We Ignore: Leadership Education in Business Schools," *Journal of Leadership Studies* 5, no. 1 (1998): 84, 85.

2

The Art of the Possible: The Archivist as Administrator

Frank G. Burke

A public officer in the United States is uniformly simple in his manners, accessible to all the world, attentive to all requests and obliging in his replies.

—Alexis de Tocqueville[1]

THE PLACE OF ARCHIVES IN THE INFORMATION PROFESSIONS

Tocqueville's ruminations apply particularly to archivists because most of us are public officers and therefore obliged to be accessible to all the world, with some exceptions. Whether all of us are simple in our manners, attentive to all requests, and obliging in our replies depends largely on our individual personalities, of course, but also to a great extent on the placement of our archives, the attitude of our work staff, and the influence and direction of our superiors.

I would argue, however, that archivists are different from their colleagues in the information-purveying field. We are not smarter, better trained, better paid, or more endowed with good manners. Our difference arises out of the material that we handle and the clientele with whom we deal on a daily basis. Except in the mega-institutions at the federal level and in some states, archives operations are smaller, more "tucked away" in odd building spaces, and, generally, less known to the public. *Everybody* needs, and goes to, libraries. School groups, scout troops, and senior citizens flock to museums for education, entertainment, or just diversion on cold days. States, counties, and municipalities provide financial support for these institutions because the public demands them. Groups form "friends of the library," individuals volunteer as docents and guides in the museums, and county councils float bond issues for their support. In the mind of most citizens (perhaps excluding genealogists) the city, county, or state archives is thought of as part of the bureaucratic mechanism of government where esoteric documents ultimately end up after being passed down from official to clerk to functionary.

Administration of archives carries more of a burden than administering an institution that deals with objects available in multiple copies. Archivists who provide reference service for their holdings must also understand their materials in both context and substance. Context provides the route to the information in a corporate structure. Substance provides the specific answers to questions that can be found only in the unique documents at hand. Indeed, the training of archivists emphasizes analysis and evaluation of evidence more than process. In such a field, *rules* are not as important as *reason*, and it is more critical to have staff who can analyze and think than staff who can learn processes and universally apply them. Archival description can come only from an examination of the material at hand after inspection and an understanding of the context in which it was created.

In this chapter I will address the role and skills of archival administrators, and I believe that it is in the different nature of archives where administration, supervision, and leadership require practices with particular application to the field.

THE STATES OF ARCHIVES IN 2000

In some ways, archivists are not burdened with old processes and procedures at a time when the information world is rocketing ahead into new realms of communication, digitization, technology in general, and entrepreneurship. Archivists are facing a time during which they can test their skills and teachings, unlike other information specialists who must face the demolition of their tried and true pre-1960s technology and formats. This is the time when archival leadership has its greatest opportunity to advance the profession.

Although large institutions come to mind when one thinks of an archival establishment, most archivists work in extremely small institutional settings. Most archives have a staff of fewer than five people; in many cases there is only one salaried member on the staff, and that person is perhaps a part-time employee. Many, if not most of the remaining archival staffs are composed of students who may or may not be paid an hourly wage, or of volunteers. Any page of the "Appendix A: Employing Institutions of Individual Members" in the *SAA Membership Directory, 1998–99*, reveals the pattern, with most institutions reporting only one member of the Society on staff. While it is true that not all working archivists are members of the Society of American Archivists (SAA). the preponderance of one-member institutions in Appendix A is a clear indication of the general state of employment in the field.

PROFESSIONAL COMMUNICATIONS

One could ask how a profession survives with members scattered in one-person shops as "lone-arrangers" throughout the country, especially when in most of these archives resources are scarce, and space, equipment, and even attention from institutional resource providers are also in short supply. Stuck in small compartments in out-of-the-way areas of the institution, the archives' activities probably have a negligible impact on the institution's mission and programs. Although every archivist, even under these circumstances, has working relationships with *somebody*, in small archives those administrative relationships are probably confined to questions of staff, facilities, and equipment.

With no on-the-job colleagues with whom they can discuss professional questions, archivists at small installations depend on their outside colleagues for advice. The number of local and regional organizations of archivists attest to how much they feel the need for consultation. The *Directory of Archival Organizations in the United States and Canada* (1997) lists eight national and forty-seven regional, state, and local archival organizations for the United States alone.[2] They are the connection to the outside world needed by archivists in institutions where there is no one else to talk to about the issues of the profession. In addition to volunteer organizations outside of the national society, the SAA itself provides opportunities for its members to join sub-groups where professional and technical concerns can be aired and exchanged. The Society's sections and round tables distribute occasional bulletins and newsletters to their members, and the Society itself publishes the primary archival professional journal quarterly: *The American Archivist*. What all of this activity represents is an attempt to dispense information of use to the professional archivist who is not in a position to communicate with colleagues at work about technical, ethical, or other professional issues. Archivists at small institutions who wish to discuss their work do so through external communication (including the Internet and various list-serves) rather than internal working relationships.

OPERATIONAL SIZE AS A FACTOR IN MANAGEMENT

Small Archival Institutions

Management in a small archives where the archival worker is also the archival manager provides little opportunity to develop managerial and leadership skills. Management of volunteers or temporary student help is an art in itself, but it does not hone one's skills in promoting incentives, professional growth, and increasing responsibility. If one of the primary roles of any manager is to train and develop one's own successors, that incentive is lacking in the small shop. Ambitious archivists who feel the need to express themselves, try out new ideas, and learn from discussion and debate, turn to the professional organizations in an attempt to share information and contribute to the greater good. There are places where a small archives is in a branch of an institution that also has a larger archives, but not many individuals fit that pattern. If the large archival institutions with their large staffs seem to be dominating the professional society, the *Directory* shows that they certainly have a large presence, but participate in leadership positions with many lone-arrangers.

A small archival institution provides excellent training in some ways, but is faulty in others. The excellent part has to do with the fact that the "lone-arranger" not only arranges or organizes materials, but must also undertake appraisal, acquisition, accessioning, analysis, description, reference, and collection maintenance duties, and perhaps even the development and maintenance of a web page. This scope of work provides end-to-end control over the material and gives the archivist a full view of what archivists do. Thus, the positive side of working in a small archival institution is that it provides an opportunity for innovation and experimentation with processes and techniques. Since the profession has been slack in agreeing on rigid standards for the format and structure of finding aids, for instance, archivists in a small shop have an opportunity to experiment with variations on what some archivists think of as "traditional" registers and inventories. Such experimentation can lead to even more chaos in the profession, except that the innovator can take his or her ideas out to the larger world through participation in the activities of the professional organizations. Most of the technical innovations that we have seen over the past thirty years have come from entrepreneurial attempts at improvement of processes, which then graduated into consideration by study groups, committees, and task forces who promoted the good ideas and spread the word to the rest of the community. Today's professional leaders were, for the most part, yesterday's young archivists who had new ideas, and now provide leadership to the profession through the SAA.

The negative part of being a lone-arranger is that under normal circumstances there is no technical oversight, no critique of the work accomplished, no second-guessing some decisions, such as records appraisal. The archives soon takes on the stamp of the archivist, for better or worse.

Large Archival Institutions

Management in a large archives provides a larger responsibility that for most people outweighs working in a small archival operation with its freedom of action, possibilities for innovation, and avoidance of supervisory problems.

My own move from a department of special collections with a staff of three and a half professionals, one clerical assistant, and a varying number of part-time student assistants, to an office of fifty staff members in a major library, where I supervised fifteen professional archivists and technicians, was not as difficult a transition as one might imagine. The comparison may be that of moving from a small town to a big city, where the scale itself is daunting. But in every big city there are neighborhoods, and in your neighborhood you are most concerned about the block you live on and the people with whom you interact on a daily basis.

Perhaps the first thing that one notices when assuming responsibilities in a large institution after serving in a small one, is the scale of resources that are available. Little things that were troublesome in the past cause few problems. Needed supplies are stockpiled instead of parceled out. Tasks are allocated so that it is not necessary to do everything one's self, thus reducing non-productive distractions. Phones are answered, letters typed, mail distributed, equipment procured and maintained by others who have those responsibilities, and advice is offered when needed.

A new supervisor in such a setting finds that the basis for all of this is order and process. Any staff member who is supervised is covered by a position description and designated duties. The parameters of the tasks at hand are outlined in statements of mission, goals, and objectives. Processes and procedures are (or should be) covered by manuals. A supervisor is expected to know what tasks are active and to oversee their accomplishment. It is much like a builder constructing a house: the plans are there, the materials are supplied, and the job is to make sure that the carpenters know where to cut, what to hammer, and when to move on to the next unit. If any new skills are required of the workers, they are offered training. It all seems so orderly and predictable that anyone could rise to be the level of supervisor. The only element left out of the manuals and policy statements is the human one.[3]

THREE SCENARIOS FOR NEW MANAGERS

New managers can come from anyplace—a transfer from another unit of an institution, promotion up through the ranks in the same unit, or from a different institution where archival duties were performed. There are advantages and disadvantages in each case. A move from another unit in the institution to an archival management position gives the manager an advantage of knowing the institution and its operating traditions. The institutional philosophy is understood, and the new manager knows the administrative hierarchy and internal procedures. A disadvantage might be that the staff will be certain to inquire about the new manager's reputation at his or her old job, and a hint of anything negative will often take months to counteract with positive actions. On the other hand, glowing reports from the past can help smooth the transition to the new relationship.

The promotion of a manager within the same archival unit can be advantageous if staff relations have been pleasant in the past, and if there is no rancor about someone else being passed over for the promotion. The new manager is at least fully aware of staff assignments and responsibilities, and what planning has been done for the immediate future. Negatively, the transition from peer to supervisor can be a difficult one, as old friendships and sympathies for another's job-related difficulties must be taken into account when evaluating the efficiency of the unit's operation. Friendships of long-standing can be strained by a new relationship, where a former colleague is now a supervisor.

An internal promotion can also have a negative effect on the new manager's ability or willingness to make changes. If "Joe" has been on the archives staff for any length of time, he is accustomed to the policies and procedures that have been established. Although he may feel that some changes would suit his style or strengthen his impact, it might be difficult to convince the staff that they are necessary, and there will be a transition period between the time when Joe is just a colleague and when he is the "boss."

But Joe should also be aware of what changes the staff have been asking for that were never implemented, or even considered. The best route for Joe to follow would be to inform the staff that he sees room for change, but would like their input before he makes any. Joe's success or failure will depend on his ability to communicate and to convince others of the validity of his arguments. If he can bring the staff around to a conviction that modifications in process, procedures, or even work assignments will be beneficial for the overall operation of the office, as well as for the individual staff members, he will have evidenced a leadership quality that will enhance his position as a colleague *and* administrator in their eyes.

The most difficult management change to predict is the one that occurs when a new unit manager comes from outside, with an unknown reputation, but legitimate credentials. Staff will anticipate changes in philosophy, processes, and maybe even assignments. Perhaps "Jill" is the successful applicant for a position at the state historical society, where she will supervise a dozen people in the manuscripts processing unit. "Jill" is finishing her doctoral dissertation at the state university, where she is a history major who has worked in the library's special collections unit as assistant curator, with a staff of four supplemented by part-time students. The new job means a move to the capital city. Jill anticipates a period of adjustment until she masters the pattern of staff relationships, understands institutional philosophy, and learns the hierarchy of authority.

On arrival, Jill finds a pleasant but cautious welcome from the staff and a supportive but hands-off superior, who is quite willing to delegate authority. One staff member obviously had applied for the job that she was awarded, and a majority of the staff members have been in place from five to ten years. When Jill looks at the products of the staff efforts she finds them to be completely different from what was produced at her old job, of lower quality, in her mind, and without regard for any of the newer techniques touted by other archives. The assignment is obviously going to be a challenge.

When Jill discusses these conditions with her old boss in special collections, she is advised to tread lightly, but firmly, until she has an understanding of the paths to take and the actions to implement. It is suggested that she turn to a knowledgeable and respected member of the staff or her retired predecessor who can provide honest and impartial assessments of the existing staff, planning scenarios, institutional relations, and other background intelligence. Armed with this knowledge, Jill schedules one-on-one "chats" with each staff member, not in her office, but in their workplace, or over a light lunch in the cafeteria. It might take a few weeks of this kind of preparation before Jill is ready to suggest to the staff that she would like to try some different approaches to the work of the unit, and asks their cooperation in some experiments. If all goes well, Jill is on the road to becoming not just an imported supervisor, but a manager who is respected and approachable.

A third scenario is that of "Jack," who worked for a number of years in a large archival institution supervising a small staff doing special projects.

Jack is promoted to administer a troubled office, where the top administration is unhappy with the current supervisor because of poor budget administration and work progress, but where there is a very loyal staff. Jack steps into a situation where his selection is resented and there are many staff communications with the deposed boss, who has been assigned irrelevant duties elsewhere as someone's "special assistant." In this case Jack knows the institution's structure and philosophy, knows what level of performance is expected and how other units are functioning, and has full support of the administration above him. After one or two weeks of staff resistance to any suggested modifications of professional behavior, Jack calls a staff meeting, admonishes the staff for their unprofessional behavior, sets out what he expects to see from them in the succeeding months, schedules performance reviews for the end of that time period, and invites any of them to sit down with him privately to discuss any matters that they wish. Requests for transfer out of the unit will be supported, new ideas will be listened to carefully, and rationality will be rekindled. Jack's approach does not guarantee success, but he is probably on the right track.

Many of us have experienced one or more of these situations. Although conditions are different in each, new experiences can only work towards a common goal, which is a pleasant work environment, a sense of direction, the satisfaction of accomplishment, and regret when relationships end as colleagues change positions and supervisors move on. But, in truth, a leader of people does not adhere to a behavioral formula, unless that formula consists of recognizing different situations and adjusting to meet them. A leader knows, perhaps instinctively, how and when to temper authority with collegiality—how to "read" a situation and act appropriately. Over a long career, the scenarios for Joe, Jill, and Jack might really be combined in the person of "Jim," as he moves from one management position to another and faces each of the three situations.

I use these scenarios because I believe that they illustrate how difficult it is to generalize any instruction about management and leadership. At the beginning of their careers, people rarely plan for management responsibilities, unless their education has been aimed specifically at that goal. Since most archivists enter the field with an education in the humanities or social sciences, they have probably had only one semester course in some kind of institutional management, but with little direct application to the type of management that they will be performing in archival institutions. Learning the principles of planning, programming, personnel, budgets, facilities, and other managerial functions is certainly important, but these must then be modified, or even twisted, in their application to specialized fields.

BASIC TENETS OF SUPERVISION AND LEADERSHIP

A good supervisor will not initiate new processes without at least some consultation with affected staff, and at best only after a joint effort to test a new procedure against the old, prove its effectiveness, and in the end have the staff members understand why the change is being made, and embrace it. If a supervisor can look at the assignment as a collegial process with an intellectual (and perhaps social) challenge, the atmosphere in an office or a stack area can be modified positively. The process can also change how such a person is perceived—as just another supervisor, or as a leader.

A large archival institution compartmentalizes most of the archival processes: appraisal, organization, description, reference, and the like are carried out by specialty staff, with occasional overlapping—such as description and reference. In a large archives the direction and oversight of the supervisor assumes considerable importance, because he or she is the funnel through which the products go, and where critiques are initiated. The role of the manager, therefore, is an active one, and the archivist-in-charge should be involved in staff consultations on acquisition, processing, description, and reference activities, and even the outreach efforts of an institutional web site. Since some of these activities, such as organizing a mass of material, may stretch out over weeks or even months for one large collection, the archivist is not involved every day in what the staff is doing, but does take part in the initial plan of organization and periodically reviews progress. In many ways, an archivist is best trained for these responsibilities through prior experience as a lone-arranger, where he or she did all of them.

The archival supervisor or manager should read in draft every finding aid that is prepared by the staff, and should sample the outgoing reference mail for style and accuracy (some supervisors insist on signing all outgoing reference letters). The supervisory archivist in a manuscript collection should be involved with prospective donors, work with staff to keep up communication, set time aside to meet with all parties, encourage prospective donors to donate, and maintain contact with donors even after a collection has been accessioned, processed, and shelved.

Managing a large archival operation thus entails more than supervising staff like a line boss in an assembly plant. Supervisors *cum* managers must also plan in order to meet their responsibilities. Planning covers a wide variety of tasks and actions that deal with the environment of the workplace and the welfare of the people in it. Most environmental and workplace concerns are ultimately expressed in a budget proposal, in which the amount of resources needed are addressed and justified to higher levels of management. Some managers may look upon a budget activity as a chore that annually distracts them from the daily work to be accomplished, but it may be the most important task that the archival manager performs. Budgets force people to think about their activities and how productive or wasteful they are. Budgets force managers to plan for contingencies, and to forecast what the present level of activity will rise to, based on known or anticipated circumstances. Budget planning forces the manager to review current functions and performance—it forces everything to come to the table and justify itself, and if it cannot, its elimination or modification have to be considered. Perhaps most important of all, however, the budget process is a direct communication with higher levels of management in the organization, and presents an opportunity to place before them the case that the archivist wishes to make. A budget proposal is one document that is certain to be read at higher levels. It is a document that can either impress or distress the decision makers, and, therefore, the budget document is something that should be thought of every working day, and not just at the end of the fiscal year. The evaluation of a manager as good, just okay, or poor, does not hinge only on his or her personality and camaraderie with the staff, but how he or she perceives past and present problems and future solutions. Management is not concerned only with individuals on the staff, but with space requirements, equipment needs to increase efficiency, morale conditions based on the working environment, training needed to upgrade skills, and incentives to reward extraordinary performance. If a budget request includes consideration of all of these elements, it may not be fully granted, but it will register with those in a position to do something about them in the future, and at least trigger a positive reaction towards a manager and staff that has a sense of priorities. A manager who works hard for the improvement of conditions will reap the rewards of an appreciative staff.

DISPLAYING LEADERSHIP THROUGH TEAMWORK

If a moderate to large organization presents opportunities for the archivist/manager to communicate with upper management, it also presents opportunities for interoffice activities that provide personal visibility, cooperative ventures with other offices, and a growing understanding of the institutional image of itself. Every university, library, large historical society, large state archives, and kindred institutions have internal committees, formed by the institution's leadership to enlarge discussion of common issues. The institutional archivist may be assigned to some of these committees, or may volunteer to be on them. An enlightened manager regards such activities as team performance, a chance for expanding knowledge, personal visibility, networking, and providing many opportunities to inform people of the functions and activities of the archives and its importance to the institution. The influence of the archival manager on other institutional committee or task force members may be only subliminal, but leadership qualities will show themselves in such a context. Person-to-person contact with other institutional members will, over time, provide easier paths to co-operation in favor of the archives' needs or programs. Onerous as it may seem at one moment, the opportunity to chair an interdepartmental committee is an "honor" that will raise the status of the archives faster than would an increased production of finding aids, albeit to a different clientele.

One of the reasons that a manager's institutional activities are important is because of his or her position between staff and upper management. The term "middle manager" is very apt, and an institutional archivist always has one eye concentrating on the staff he or she supervises, and the other focusing on the organization's hierarchy. The archivist is continually representing one side to the other, by explaining and justifying the archives staff activities to superiors, and clarifying upper-management policies and practices to the archives staff. Service on committees and task forces throughout the institution enhances a manager's ability to communicate bilaterally between the archives staff and the institution at large. In many ways, the enlarged activities undertaken by the institutional archivist within the parent institution ensures enhanced personal effectiveness outside the institution. We are all called upon to address groups about our work and our programs, most often, perhaps, at professional meetings. Awareness of the larger picture of our institution makes it easier for us to convey why we do certain things in the archives, our policies and practices, and our relations with other institutions. Conversely, an archivist's participation in professional organizations provides a broader knowledge of how things are done elsewhere, which can buttress requests for change in procedures in one's own institution.

INNOVATION IN AN ARCHIVAL BUREAUCRACY

My earlier statement indicates that small archival offices have opportunities to innovate processes and procedures, largely unfettered by corporate or agency restrictions. This is not to imply that innovation does not occur at large institutions. Indeed, large institutions generally have better resources of funds and equipment that can be used for experimentation. But larger archives have more compartmentalized tasks than do smaller institutions. Staff in a major archives will specialize in appraisal, accessioning, reference, processing, or editing finding aids. In each of these areas there are daily tasks to accomplish, either by plan or in reaction to researcher needs and demands. It is unlikely that one staff member would depart from assigned duties and try experimenting with a new computer programming idea, or that one who is preparing finding aids would produce a revolutionary new format just to see how it is received. Tasking, scheduling, and supervising tend to dampen such unscheduled individual initiatives.

A good manager recognizes, however, that there may *be* alternatives to current procedures. Perhaps an idea comes from a staff member as a suggestion for change. The supervisor could quash the initiative by citing extant procedures manuals, tradition, or lack of time to experiment. A better manager would ask the entrepreneurial staff member to take a little time to write up the ideas, and promise a review by other staff and managers. A small ad hoc committee would be established, the proposal circulated, a discussion session held, and the proponent given a chance to elaborate on the proposal and respond to questions or lead a discussion of possibilities.

If an idea for change is not original with a staff member, but something that is brought back from a professional meeting in a report about another institution's innovations, the archival manager may appoint a contact person or set up a small committee on communication, so that there can be an exchange of information with the outside innovator. It may be that reciprocal visits are arranged between the two archives and other institutions involved, with plans to meet at the next professional meeting. The process is not novel, and it describes the reality of how the archival profession has advanced in the fields of photocopying, preservation, software development, electronic records, and other process innovations.

A good manager encourages suggestions for innovation, and looks for resources that will support further study and development. A good manager involves others in developing grant applications to federal and private agencies, first, in order to fund the experiments, and second, to draw the attention of upper management to the initiatives of the archival unit. A secure manager will not worry that one of his staff is being credited with innovation and advancement of the profession, because the reputation of the entire archival unit will be enhanced when it attracts national attention, even in its relatively small professional field. The difference between a large and a small archives is that at the former, ideas must go through a review and approval process before any resources are expended (including staff time) on a new idea.

GETTING HELP FOR THE ARCHIVES

Archival managers are not confined only to operational supervision, since there is another element in intra-institutional relations that can sometimes be necessary, at least under extraordinary circumstances. There are many archives that operate in a political climate, from the National Archives and Records Administration to local historical societies. The term of the politically appointed director may not be long enough for an archivist or society director to establish rapport with the overseeing agency or administration. The director and staff of the archival institution may feel ignored, isolated, misunderstood, unappreciated, or, what is worse, subject to excessive interference by the administration. Some state archives are within the state library system; some are part of the state historical society; others report to the secretary of state. There may come a time when continued neglect or professional interference from any of these upper levels are having a negative effect on the ability of the archivist to perform the duties of the office efficiently and professionally. The most egregious sin is for the top administrator to begin appointing unqualified functionaries to positions in the archives or historical society. A lesser adverse action, but just as damaging, is for administrators to ignore the archives' budgetary needs on a systematic basis and possibly reduce the budget for unexplained or inappropriate fiscal reasons. Administrative "raids" on one's resources, including space, are threats that need immediate attention, before they result in total deconstruction of the archival program.

One of the remedies sought by many archives managers in difficult political situations is to find friendly members of the faculty senate, historical society board of trustees, county council, or the state or federal legislature, as applicable, and enlist their support in bringing some pressure on the threatening parties to rethink negative decisions or patronage. The direct intervention of an archives director in a political process can be very dangerous, both to the archivist and to the institution. High-level administrators do not like being pressured on what they may perceive as a petty problem coming from a petty employee. For these and other reasons it is desirable to have an archives advisory council, or a "friends of the archives" group in place, made up of individuals who represent the constituency of the archives, largely or wholly outside of government or the home institution. It is commonly understood that advisory councils are not appointed just to give advice, but also to act as a conduit to those who can help the program, and/or as a buffer between the archives and forces that threaten its stability, including budget stability. Some government levels prohibit the establishment of advisory groups without approval from the administration. In the federal system the Office of Management and Budget (OMB) has strict regulations on this issue—especially if there will be any expenditure of funds for meetings. The restrictions have not stopped managers from forming interagency committees as sounding boards, and even including local professionals who provide a *pro bono* contribution. State archivists have at their disposal the NHPRC-created State Historical Records Advisory Board (SHRAB), composed of archivists, historians, records managers, librarians, elected and appointed government officials, and other professionals. Board members serve as unpaid appointees not only to review records grant applications in their states, but also to coordinate the overall strategies for improving archival and record keeping functions within the state. At the time of the creation of the SHRABS, the Executive Director of the NHPRC stated:

[T]he Advisory Board might become the chief lobbyist, so to speak, for all those in the States concerned about the preservation and use of historical records. This effort might be focused especially on the State government, but could also extend, as needed, to local governments, to key organizations and institutions, to sources of financial support, and to the regional and federal level.[4]

Almost all government employees, at all levels of government, are prohibited from lobbying, or promoting their own cause to the legislative body or board that oversees them. However, members of an advisory board who are not affiliated with the archival agency can act as intermediaries between the archives and those who have the authority to act for relief or enhancement of the institution. Members of advisory bodies are appointed because of their interest in the institution and its work, but also because they may be in a position to publicize its needs. Members may also be able to act as an intermediary when there are political storm clouds, and plead the institution's case when errors occur or a finger of blame is being unjustly pointed at it. Additionally, the archivist can turn to such a body for advice before undertaking something that may have political or organizational objections. Finally, if the advisory body can wrest some power to itself, it might be granted authority to be constituted as a "search committee" when the top position at the archives is to be filled, and recommend two or three well qualified candidates from which the administration can select one. Some of the problems at NARA over the first ten years of independence after 1985 stemmed from the absence of such a screening committee for the selection of Archivist of the United States. Two acting archivists held the office for a total of five years, while the appointing body (the White House) failed to identify appropriate candidates. Such indecision could have been averted if there had been a professional screening panel. It is not just the largest archival institutions that need such devices as advisory bodies: archival administrators can use the assistance of well-chosen panels at all levels of the profession.

The most extreme example of action to alleviate intolerable institutional relationships is that of the National Archives independence movement of the 1980s. Directed by Robert Warner, who was appointed Archivist of the United States in 1980, the movement resulted four years later in the establishment of the National Archives and Records Administration (NARA) as an independent agency. The story is too long to tell here, but it has been detailed in Warner's book *Diary of a Dream: A History of the National Archives Independence Movement, 1980–1985* (Scarecrow Press, 1995). For archivists, the book is the equivalent of Machiavelli's *The Prince*, except that Warner does not just speculate on how to deal with a difficult bureaucrat, he relates how it was successfully carried out. Every archival manager should read it for the lessons that Warner shares with us.[5] Not everyone could have done what he did, but then, not everyone exhibits the kind of leadership that Warner displayed throughout his archival career. He would be the first to warn, however, that not all grievances demand drastic counteractions. A professional leader knows how and when to compromise, to negotiate, to work towards improving a bad situation, or, in cases dealing with elected or short-term officials, when to wait them out and when to begin presenting one's case to the incoming successor. Unfortunately, and almost inexplicably, the concept of an Archives Advisory Council was not included in the NARA enabling act of 1984. In hard times, the Archivist may have to face difficulties alone.

THE NATURE OF ARCHIVAL ADMINISTRATION AND LEADERSHIP

If I were to paraphrase the Tocqueville quote at the beginning of this chapter, I would cast it as follows:

An archival administrator in the United States is uniformly pleasant in manner, accessible to all the staff, attentive to all their needs, and undaunted in pursuit of the best tools for the tasks at hand.

Any administrator who can follow through on those criteria will be a leader, and yet the elements of leadership are not confined to organizational and material matters. A true leader excels in personal attributes that expand the Golden Rule, and true leaders have been with us for millennia, most frequently working within organizational systems that demanded skills, innovation, foresight, empathy, equitability, maturity of mind, abnegation of self, and, perhaps, a touch of panache. True leaders are not new, and we can find them in institutions large and small. If we think back on our own training in the archival field archivists will remember some administrators more fondly than others. The qualities that we remember relate largely to how they treated us and others who worked with us. In some cases they inspired us through their confidence, which was not bravado; they confronted obstacles and sought solutions; they were collegial without being patronizing; they were competitive and wanted to make our facility the best of its kind, large or small. Good administrators regularly wandered through our work area, not "checking up" but exhibiting a true curiosity about how our tasks were going and interest in new materials we had discovered; or they sat quietly in the back of the room as we made a presentation to others or conducted meetings—not to criticize, but to learn and perhaps to offer hints afterwards. Leaders at all levels give high priority to their jobs, their staff, and their relationships with others. If they are lone-arrangers they may turn these attributes to bear on professional activities outside of their shop; they are connected and communicative, and in later years we dedicate our books to the memory of their guidance. If we look back on the leaders in our profession we find that not all were administrators of large archives; not all had a large body of writings to their credit; not all were dynamic speakers or sparkling conversationalists; but they all had an aura about them that made us stop and listen when they spoke, and yearn to emulate their manner if we were given an opportunity to rise to positions of leadership in the profession. Most leaders did not seek a leadership position: leaders are *recognized*, not made. We are what we are as a profession because of them.

It is a strange but indisputable fact that leaders are not always right, or ultimately successful, or unquestionably honored. Institutions sometimes have views that are different from those of the knowledgeable public. Leaders can sometimes alienate or dismay their superiors by adherence to professional standards for retention of records. Not every corporation administrator (or lawyer) agrees with the archivist about preserving his or her files and papers and making them available to the public. Not all institutional directors are sympathetic to their archivist's desire to retain materials relating to institutional failures, even though the archivist's argument is supportive of historical fact. Not all research institutions concur with the archivist's decision to retain papers of someone the faculty or administration consider to be controversial, or criminal. Not all archivists are praised for seeking more space for at-risk collections if there is competition for it by a unit of higher public visibility. Archivists who wish to broaden their professional standing through scholarly publication are often restrained by an institution that will not grant time to do so. Not all archival leaders are appointed to appropriate positions when politics or the spoils system override rationality and professionalism. It is, after all, the keeper of the flame who is most likely to be the one who gets burned. Fortunately, some of our colleagues who have fallen in the wars of politics and ego have risen to their true calling elsewhere, honored by their peers as leaders in the profession.

Having opened this chapter with a quote from 165 years ago, I thought I would close with one from something older, to show how the human spirit has been with us for millennia. In the second century, A.D., the Stoic philosopher Marcus Aurelius began to set down his philosophy of life by citing all of the personal attributes that he had learned from his family, friends, colleagues, and especially his [adoptive] father, Emperor Antonius Pius.

In my father I learned mildness of temper, and unchangeable resolution in the things which are determined after due dilberation; and no vainglory in those things which men call honors, and a love of labor and perseverance; and a readiness to listen to those who had anything to propose for the common weal; and undeviating firmness in giving to every man according to his deserts, and a knowledge derived from experience of the occasions for vigorous action and for remission. . . . I observed, too, his habit of careful inquiry in all matters of deliberation, and his persistency, and that he never stopped his investigation through being satisfied with appearances which first present themselves, and that his disposition was to keep his friends, and not to be soon tired of them, not yet to be extravagant in his affection; and to be satisfied on all occasions, and cheerful; and to forsee things a long way off, and to provide for the smallest without display; and to check immediately popular applause and flattery; and to be ever watchful over the things that were necessary for the administration of the empire; and to be a good manager of the expenditure, and patiently to endure the blame which he got for such conduct.[6]

Here are aphorisms that could inspire our professional leaders even today, and illustrate how concepts of leadership have not significantly changed in two thousand years.

NOTES

1. Alexis de Tocqueville, *Democracy in America* (New York: Vintage Press, 1954), I, 214–215.

2. This is published by the Society of American Archivists and included as an insert in their newsletter *Archival Outlook* from time to time. I am using the one from the May/June 1997 issue.

3. There is a good section dealing with managing professionals, peers, and helping employees succeed in Thomas Wilsted and William Nolte, *Managing Archival and Manuscript Repositories* (Chicago: Society of American Archivists, 1991), 42–44. In these and other pages of the work, however, managers and employees are characterized more in conflict than in harmony.

4. "NHPRC Agenda," Meeting of State Historical Records Coordinators, July 22, 1976, F.G. Burke Personal Records, *Speeches and Writings* file, "Remarks," p. 3.

5. My only hesitation is that the book is not really a *history*; it is a *diary*, moderately annotated. A history would include reference to the actions of others who

worked on the campaign with Warner. For his own protection he was not made aware of everything that his colleagues were doing.

6. Marcus Aurelius Antonius [A.D. 121–180], *Meditations*. George A. Long, translator (New York: A.L. Burt Company, n.d.), 136–137.

3

Ways and Means: Thinking and Acting to Strengthen the Infrastructure of Archival Programs

Larry J. Hackman

INTRODUCTION

Archivists typically give highest priority to their holdings and to what methods should be applied to effectively identify, acquire and preserve them and make them accessible. Less attention is given to the critical "carrier" of the archives over time, the archival program. It is the program, however, that must be sufficient into the distant future if the archival materials are to survive and be administered effectively. That is why leaders of archival programs, and individual archivists working in them, must give high priority to ways and means to strengthen the infrastructure of their programs for the long run.

The ways of thinking and acting described here draw on my experience as an observer and director of programs, not from a careful review of the literature on leadership or other aspects of program development. I have been fortunate to have had several good observation and action posts from which to learn. In the late sixties and early seventies, I conducted research on and talked extensively with many key national leaders in government, politics, and public affairs as an interviewer and then director for the John F. Kennedy Library oral history program. I learned most of all from my research and interviews that there is no one right way to do things, but that there are many productive approaches that can be applied to achieve results. Then, as the first director of the records grant program at the National Historical Publications and Records Commission (NHPRC) from 1975–81, I had the opportunity to observe the condition of many archival programs across the nation and the practices of their directors and staffs. During these years, we faced at NHPRC the related challenges of how to maximize the impact of the limited funds available to grant to these programs and also how to increase the federal appropriation that supported these grants. I learned that many archival programs lacked strong infrastructure and that many of them did not have leaders who, if ambitious for their program, also had the confidence and skills to fulfill its potential. I came to believe that planning, assessment and a high respect for archival professionalism, linked to aggressive leadership and highly leveraged resources, could lead to major progress in individual programs.

When in 1981 it seemed to me that the NHPRC was unlikely to be able to expand its impact for a period of time, I had the chance to become director of a still nearly new New York State Archives. This gave me the opportunity to test many of the methods that I had encouraged others to use during my years at NHPRC, especially strategic planning, internal and external advocacy, public relations, and a variety of high risk/high leverage approaches. During my time in New York we greatly strengthened and expanded the New York State Archives, which became the New York State Archives and Records Administration, and advanced considerably on a very broad statewide agenda for archives. I confirmed, at least for myself, that there are indeed many ways to address an ambitious agenda, particularly with the help of influential allies, including those who would be served by improved archives and records programs or who represented or identified with these beneficiaries. Finally, from 1995–2000, as director of the Truman Library and president of the Truman Library Institute, its non-profit partner, I was able to apply many of these same approaches in a very different setting, and to lead a public-private partnership in planning, and acquiring funds for, a $24 million renovation and reinvention project. Here I learned that a compelling vision for the future, and very active outreach to community leaders, can engage influential individuals and organizations, even for a forty-year-old program that had not previously involved them or attempted anything nearly so ambitious. The Truman Library experience reaffirmed for me, in a setting quite different from my prior experience, the effectiveness of many of the principles and techniques discussed below.[1]

In the first section below, I try to distill a few of the underlying ways of thinking that I have found useful to advance programs. The second section describes some particular kinds of actions to help develop a stronger infrastructure for archival programs. The distinction between ways of thinking and ways of doing is imprecise, and some of the approaches I describe could have been placed in the other category. While program directors or would-be directors are the natural audience for the ideas here, I hope that the perspective will be informative and provocative for other archivists as well.

A MINDSET TOWARD PROGRAM DEVELOPMENT: TEN WAYS OF THINKING

Certain ways of thinking about programs seem especially appropriate for program directors and other individuals who share responsibility for the future of archival programs. In my opinion, all archivists working within a given archival program share in the responsibility for program development, along with their professional responsibilities more narrowly defined, because all have a responsibility to contribute to the future management and accessibility of the records held by their institution. Program development goes faster and better when the staff understands its importance and participates in and supports it with enthusiasm. It is the director of an archival program, however, who has a particular obligation to make program development her or his primary responsibility from the very first, and who must regularly reassess the state of the program's infrastructure and develop the action plans to strengthen it. Ordinarily both the director and those who make the appointment should make this responsibility very clear at the time the director is selected.[2]

Here are some of the ways of thinking that, in retrospect, seem to have helped me advance the programs which I have directed and to strengthen them for continuing effectiveness:

1. The primary test for success is not the present, it's the future. The state of a program cannot be assessed adequately from a snapshot of the program at a particular point. My task as a program developer is to create conditions so that the program performs effectively now and, most importantly, has or is moving rapidly toward what it needs to sustain and improve that performance in the future. I like to think that in each of my major assignments I have improved the performance of the program I encountered and, upon departing it, have left in place many of the key elements of infrastructure needed for the years ahead, or a strong base and good momentum for obtaining them. I would expect my successors, and those who hired me, to assess my contribution by comparing the program's infrastructure to its condition when I arrived—but especially by considering its adequacy for the future.

2. The program infrastructure counts the most. Archivists naturally view archival programs mainly in terms of the quality and status of hold-

ings, the soundness and currency of archival methods, the number and type of users, and the products of research in the archives. These are all very important indicators of performance. From a broader (and longer) perspective, however, the key indicators are the soundness, sufficiency, and sustainability of key elements required by any strong program in any field. This includes systems for governance, direction, planning, and evaluation; policies regarding administration and personnel; procedures and techniques to be applied in the main activities of the program; advisors, supporters, and partners; financial resources and control of their use; facilities; staffing and staff development; and the overall organizational climate, including internal and external expectations for the quality and scope of the program. When any of these are not strong, we cannot be confident that archival functions will be executed effectively on a continuing basis.

3. Patience is not golden, but patience is necessary. Good program developers are impatient and ambitious for their programs. They want a lot to happen, and the sooner the better. Major breakthroughs, however, usually don't happen quickly, regardless of the energy and imagination brought to the task. Important change, change that is likely to have long-term positive impact on the health of a program, usually depends on a prior period of analysis, goal setting, identifying appropriate strategies and tactics, building key relationships, developing formal proposals, and then advocating them thoughtfully and energetically. Often much of this is taking place behind the scenes, and often it's not entirely obvious, even to the program developer, that the pieces are falling in place. Patience will be rewarded—if wise actions are being taken to put the springs and levers in place that can produce the major changes desired. In the meantime, credibility and respect must be built every day along the way through performance, service, and good communication with those who are critical to success.

4. An agenda with sound strategies is better than a detailed plan. To bring about major change means to be prepared to seize opportunities, and to do that means having a sense of the broad goals that the program seeks ultimately to address on an ongoing basis. The basic elements of a good strategic planning process are immensely helpful in reexamining mission, developing a compelling vision, identifying issues critical to success, and setting main objectives and strategies to address them. But seizing opportunities is difficult if the program has adopted and feels bound by a highly detailed plan with assignments, actions, and deadlines. Such plans often take on a life of their own and can keep the program leadership from seeing and seizing opportunities.[3] A detailed plan can be a trap, unless a very strong capacity already exists to carry it out, including resources and the

commitments of key players—in which case one may suspect that the main criteria for the plan is being "safe" rather than strategic.

5. <u>Personal security and maximum program development cannot both be the highest priority.</u> Program developers/directors should make no permanent personal plans! The test to be met is not survival, it's to optimize positive impact—and then to step aside if needed. Some very talented people can manage to do both very well over a long period of time—but they are the exception. I found, for example, after a period of great progress in New York, that among the most important challenges remaining were aspects of state information technology policy and practice. I knew that these were neither my strength nor my passion, and I felt that a change in leadership would likely be positive for the State Archives and Records Administration. More recently at the Truman Library, after more than five years of rapid change, highlighted by a successful major capital campaign, renovation and program expansion, the work ahead included the day to day management of programs and staff and the transformation of resource development from capital campaign to an ongoing program of underwriting and annual and planned giving. Again, I felt I would not sustain the high energy and wise patience that these activities required, and so it seemed best to prepare the way for new leadership who could provide these while taking advantage of the high community interest and the momentum established during my tenure.

6. There is no one right place for the archives when considered across time. Most archival programs are part of something larger—a library, historical society, a corporate body of some sort—and a number of effective placements and combinations with other functions can be effective. It's useful to think of the archival program in relation to the larger entity in its largest form—corporation wide, university system wide, government wide. <u>While the archival function must not be compromised, often the way to strengthen it is within an enlarged program which includes additional functions.</u> Archival program developers should actively consider the possibility of combining the archival program with related functions. This might make sense especially if: (a) the performance of these functions is important to your success anyway; (b) the combined functions have a strong possibility of bringing a resource level to the overall combined enterprise that will make the archival function stronger; or (c) the other function or functions brings high interest or respect from internal management or influential external parties that, if drawn upon, could get vital cooperation important to performing the archival function effectively. While change in placement may seem a frightening possibility, such change is likely to be less desirable if it is entirely upon

the initiative of others, rather than something considered, prepared for, or even proposed by the archival program itself.

7. A little subject matter and technical knowledge can go a long way for a program director. As the director, I need not be an expert but should strive for "sufficiency." I need to focus on program development, not on mastering the subject matter in the archives, or on being an expert in archival methods. Turning to staff for knowledge of methods and content makes both the director and the staff more effective in most cases. The best leader for an archival program often may not be an archivist at all, but someone who, understanding archival value and grasping principles at a basic level, can focus especially on building up the entire program infrastructure and giving special attention to those elements that are impeding archival work, or might well do so in the future.

8. Examine and reexamine; think and rethink. As a program developer, I need also to make certain that the elements so critical to program success are regularly reexamined. Those that need to be refined and strengthened should be highlighted and brought to the attention of both internal and external parties who can help improve and maintain them. Whatever the circumstance, however, the underlying questions are always: (1) What is the condition of the infrastructure in relation to supporting the mission and goals of the archival program? (2) What needs to change for the infrastructure to be sufficient for the long term? (3) How can this change be brought about?

The analysis suggested here is very similar to that involved in good strategic planning, which may also identify the need for major change. This includes a review and clarification of mission and vision and institutional values, analysis of strengths and weaknesses, and a scan of the environment to identify barriers and opportunities. Especially important is the identification of the critical issues that must be addressed to achieve the mission, and the adoption of goals and strategies to address them.

As a general proposition, it is useful to hold almost nothing sacred regarding a program, to take a zero-based approach to analysis, and to invite individuals beyond the program itself to help it think outside the box about future possibilities, including radical departures from the present model.

9. Professional archival values and methods are essential. None of the ways of thinking and doing described in this article imply that sound archival practice carried out by highly qualified professional archivists is not required. It is, and not just because the materials and the users deserve it. No archival program can gain or sustain the respect and support needed without impressive knowledge and convincing performance by archival staff. And no staff will provide that unless their professional values are respected and their professional knowledge is recognized and regularly enhanced. So

professionalism underlies everything else, makes it possible, and is ultimately the most important resource to draw on for program development.

10. Toward "a thing that goes of itself." In trying to build program infrastructure adequate for the future, I have found a useful construct in the old idea of a perpetual motion device—of creating "a thing that will go of itself" to borrow the phrase that James Russell Lowell applied to the United States Constitution. While no program really can achieve such a condition, this concept has helped me to give priority to elements that can serve as continuing dynamic forces on behalf of high performance and as barriers to the "winding down" of a program. I include in these a culture of high internal and external expectations; established systems for evaluation, strategic planning, and reporting; provision for the continuing use of strong advisory groups and outside experts; and, where possible, at least partial support for the archival program from a reliable revenue stream that is not subject to annual appropriations or allocations by parties beyond the program itself. Anything that can serve as a continuing force against atrophy and that provides continuing pressure for improving infrastructure is devoutly to be desired.

WAYS OF ACTING: EIGHT SUGGESTIONS

As I reexamine my experience in several settings, I find that I have often applied the series of approaches described below to help bring about substantial change in the condition of programs. None is unique to archival programs or settings. Most will seem very obvious, and perhaps simplistic. There is a good deal of overlap among items on my list and with the "ways of thinking" described in the prior section. The challenge, of course, is in the doing. Here are some of the techniques that have worked for me:

First, enhance the perception of the quality of the program and/or its leadership by bringing achievements, especially surprising or dramatic achievements, to the attention of key individuals important to the program. Sometimes much can be done with a single event, for example, a $1 million bequest dedicated to preservation and access, the appointment of a highly distinguished individual to an advisory or governing board, receipt of a major award from the SAA or another professional association, the acquisition of the papers of a major international figure or organization, or architect's designs for a new addition to the archives. Programs need to make the most out of such developments, and many smaller ones, especially by bringing them to the attention of significant individuals who might be surprised and impressed—and therefore more likely to be supportive. But more likely a rising benchmark of credibility and visibility will be achieved through an ongoing effort to bring each significant achievement effectively to the attention of a carefully considered audience of individuals and organizations.

Much of this is just plain hard work: drafting press releases, developing mailing lists, writing letters, making appointments with people who can be helpful, reporting to the president or chairman of the organization and to members of its board, and so on. Where possible, these communications need to be particularized and personalized, even with just a brief handwritten comment on, for example, a newsletter or press release, so that the achievement is brought to the personal attention of the most influential individuals who can act on behalf of the program. This technique often will not produce dramatic results in the short run, but is almost certain to do so over time. Also, as time goes by, the old benchmark becomes the new threshold, and the audience raises its expectations for what the program should be achieving. At some point you will have established for your staff and for higher levels of administration and governance a sense that "the world is watching" your program, and this can be very useful. While it may seem frightening, it is precisely what needs to happen both inside and outside if the program is to be able to demand and obtain the resources needed to reach its potential.

High and rising expectations drive program development. Establishing a culture of high expectations for a program on the part of people internal and external to that program is highly important. It stretches the staff to perform; it stretches the organization to support; it stretches external parties to advocate when their high expectations are not met.

Second, find influential allies and secure their involvement on behalf of the program. This is crucial to most major change, especially to a meaningful expansion of continuing resources. From my observations, archival managers often set their sights too low in seeking such allies, because of a lack of confidence in their own persuasiveness or in the value of their program. Attracting "significant others," like so many things, may initially take considerable thought and effort, and a degree of serendipity is often involved. But opportunities arise where there is continued effort and, once a handful of allies is found, they will help bring others. Success is made easier by aggressively using the kinds of achievements described in the first point above.

There are a thousand possibilities for such allies: the spouse or close friend of the head of the institution; a corporate leader who has a strong interest in the subject matter or the larger institution for which the archives holds vital evidence; a well placed legislator interested in history or education or information management; an established philanthropist or newly wealthy citizen whose family or favorite hobby is documented in the archives. The first step in most of these relationships is simply to inform the individual about materials, developments or issues that might be of interest, and to probe for possible interest in broader aspects of the archival program. Usually there is a logical next step, or more than one: adding the person to the newsletter list; an invitation to a program or reception; an offer to give the individual and a group of friends a special tour or presentation; a request to join an advisory committee; a request for an introduction to another "significant other." Sometimes the "prospect" will not prove responsive; sometimes the interest can be drawn on only later, once peers have become involved in the program. But allies who can make a difference through influence and resources will only be found if the need for them is recognized and if the program director (and his colleagues) constantly seek to identify them and develop relationships with them. No program can afford not to regularly increase its circle of friends in high places, and then to bring them to appropriate advocacy on behalf of the program.[4]

Third, and this is closely related to the above, establish and maintain awareness and understanding at the highest level of management and governance. There are many ways to do this—including bringing good news, or bad news, or the demands of external parties to this highest level. An important objective is to establish a regular channel of communication at this high level, through a periodic meeting, visits to the archives, service on an archives visiting committee, or in some other way. An excellent way to initially establish interest is to have information about the archives conveyed by peers, or near peers, of the senior parties rather than from the program itself. Especially effective is contact with the senior institutional leader from someone who is not expected to be knowledgeable or enthused about the archival program but indicates that they are and will continue to be so. This sort of intervention should be sought out and, when it happens, it should then be seized upon by the program director who might suggest a way for the senior official to be kept informed on a regular basis.

Fourth, use external professional expertise for evaluation and ideas, to provide an objective "expert" description of conditions, and to recommend actions and support needed for the archival program. Consultation by experienced and respected professionals can be a valuable tool for program development. Program managers need unbiased critiques of present performance by expert professionals and their suggestions for how things can be improved. It is useful to seek external consultants who can consider not only archival methods but also assess the broader issues of management, the sufficiency and use of resources, external and internal relations, and so on. Such critiques can be useful to the archival manager in assessing his own performance, in communicating with staff about overall conditions, and also by giving credibility to information supplied to higher level administrators and resource allocators and to selected external allies about the condition of the program and its need for additional resources or other forms of support.

The archival program developer needs to consider carefully who to select as the external consultant or the leader of the external team, seeking someone who has breadth and sophistication as well as technical competence. This key individual needs to be willing and able to work closely and confidentially with the program manager so that the evaluation report (several versions of it may be needed) can be used to maximum effect to improve internal management and also to seek understanding and support from above and beyond the program itself. In almost every case, an external consultant will conclude that the archival program can improve its management and methods and needs additional resources and other support from its parent organization. The effective program developer will acknowledge areas in which change is needed, affirm her or his intention to address these, and will share this, along with the identification of resource needs, with higher level administrators and external allies. Establishing a reputation for seeking evaluation, taking it seriously, and communicating its findings and recommendations is a highly effective way to establish respect and gain support. Archival programs suffer when leaders are too timid to seek and use external evaluation and advice.

Fifth, develop an attractive "case statement," and perhaps other publications, to articulate the value and character of the program. These materials should be used aggressively to inform and impress key audiences and potential allies. One of these needs to perform the core functions of a fund raising case statement, for example, it needs to describe why the program is important, what its present condition is, how it can become more valuable and effective, and what resources and other actions are needed to fulfill its potential. The case also needs to be made as to why archival documentation is valuable to society and the ways in which the particular archives and its holdings can be used to benefit the public—and especially the particular constituencies valued by the institution at hand. Often it is wise to feature important supporters or well-known and highly respected individuals as spokespersons to make the "case" in such publications.

These basic materials should be used to secure or solidify relationships with allies and advocates. They must be well written, imaginative, and attractively designed and printed. They "stand" for the quality and the expectations of the program and communicate its core message.[5]

Sixth, seek external financial support from sources beyond the institution
of which the archives is a part and seek internal resources through means beyond the established budgeting system. Increasing resources through the established internal budget system deserves the highest priority of the
program developer, and provides the greatest prospect of continuing support; however, it is usually highly useful to also obtain resources from external organizations and individuals. Doing so can: (a) demonstrate to higher
management levels that external parties are interested in the program and
agree that it needs additional resources; (b) gain resources for key program
development activities for which internal sources cannot be obtained; (c)
provide resources that may be used more flexibly than those obtained through
internal appropriations; (d) initiate a relationship with an influential external
organization that might provide support over a period of years, or whose
members might do so, as they become acquainted with the archives; (e) test
the soundness and attractiveness of the program's basic "case" for support.

In addition to seeking external funds, it is likewise useful to search for a
new "dedicated" revenue stream from a source close to home. While this is
not always possible, a program director needs to regularly brainstorm such
possibilities. It can be immensely helpful to have a portion, ideally a major
portion, of resources from a reliable and predictable source that does not
depend on the outcome of the annual internal budget process or on a competitive search for external grants. Many archival programs have an opportunity, sometime during their life, to seek such a revenue stream via a
special fee, tax, assessment, or formula allocation. [6]

Seventh, when seeking outside financial resources, look first for high leverage for program development rather than for maximum dollars for basic program support. Many archives apply for grant funds to supplement
existing resources for basic collections processing, and this is usually appropriate. But in seeking any external support, archivists should consider
first the potential opportunities for program development leverage offered
by the application and granting process. For example, a grant for $25,000 to
support program assessment and planning, especially with a report on the
critical issues and resource needs, is much more likely to strengthen the
program than a grant of the same amount for collection processing. Sometimes seeking external funding to permit a program to prepare a highly impressive publication, multi-media production or public program, can help
obtain attention and respect that are important intermediate steps on the
way to obtaining greater internal support.

Similarly, it can be highly useful to obtain a conditional grant offer that
requires some action on behalf of the recipient (and its parent program), for
example, matching funds or, better yet, the creation of a new permanent

staff position. Such opportunities ought to be sought rather than resisted. Archival managers can often work with a grant program or individual donor to frame a conditional offer of support that will require desirable action by the larger organization in which the archives is located. Sometimes a similar result can be achieved when the granting agency rejects a grant application, and sends the applicant the message that the reason for rejection is an inappropriate policy or inadequate support from the institution in which the archives is located. This sort of high leverage support should be pursued when it might lead to increased understanding or support from the parent program—even if it also produces certain discomfort in internal relationships. In order to strengthen a program, respect is much more valuable than affection, and increased continuing support is more important than a tension-free environment.

Eighth, avoid tangential projects, no matter how "interesting" they are personally, or how "free" they appear to be, unless you can conclude that they have high potential to strengthen your program for the long run. Resources, even major resources, should not be taken for projects that, no matter how "nice to do," are likely to lead the program away from rather than toward underlying goals and a stronger infrastructure. Being able to separate means and ends is crucial. In a program development context, "projects" ought usually to be viewed as means, not ends. This is a tricky matter because, in fact, many projects can be carried out in a way that benefits rather than detracts from the program. "Special" projects ought to be viewed first as potential tools for building support, attention, respect, and alliances. The payoff for the program needs to be greater than the project costs, because even "fully funded" projects draw time and attention from basic program activities. At the Truman Library, we sponsored a major Fourth of July celebration for several years when it was crucial to raise our profile in Greater Kansas City and to establish the Library in the public mind as a place that sponsored highly successful entertaining events with demonstrable appeal to a very broad audience. Doing this took considerable effort by staff and volunteers and required separate fund raising. As soon I judged our objective had been accomplished to a sufficient degree, we passed what was widely regarded as a very successful project on to other sponsors, because its benefits to the Library no longer outweighed the costs to the Library. This special project had contributed significantly to program development in the short term, but it would not do so on a continuing basis.

CONCLUSION

Who more than archivists, who manage the documentation of the development of institutions over long spans of time, should appreciate the importance of strong organizational infrastructures able to support and sustain the archival program into the future? Who more than archivists, who deal with the records of diverse organizations from different periods of history, should be able to think clearly and creatively about what is needed to ensure the future of the programs in which they work? For it is the archival program that carries the archival materials through time and which must be able to support and apply sound archival methods. It is the archival program that needs to be developed at every point in time so that it is effective in the present and has high promise to be so in the future.

The director of each archives, working with all others who are also responsible for or care about the program, must act with them to build, maintain, and constantly enhance the infrastructure of the archival program so that sound archival practice can be sustained. The archival community, including professional associations and archival education programs, needs to give more attention to helping archivists value the importance of program development and identify and understand ways of thinking and acting appropriate to such development.[7]

NOTES

1. I have described elsewhere many of the methods that I and my colleagues employed to produce major change in the archival infrastructure for New York state during the 1980s. See especially, Larry J. Hackman "State Government and Statewide Archival Affairs: New York as a Case Study," *American Archivist* 55 (Fall 1992): 578–599. While the title is not indicative of it, this article describes not only what happened in New York, but also much about how it was done, including a separate section on "Attitudes and Approaches."

Although several useful articles have been published recently about the development of the NHPRC's records grant program (see especially the several articles in the Spring/Summer 2000 issue of *The American Archivist*), the records program's use of high leverage approaches to the development of individual archival programs has not received much attention. In fact, a thoughtful analysis of the impact of public and private grants on the basic infrastructure of individual archival programs would be very useful.

I am beginning a case study of the development of the Truman Library, and its productive partnership with the Truman Library Institute, during the period 1995–2000.

2. While the status of a program and the sufficiency of its infrastructure for the future can be reexamined at any time, it is important for a new director to conduct her or his own preliminary and personal assessment while considering whether to accept the responsibility to direct a program; a more formal agenda and strategies for action should follow early in his or her incumbency. The product of a session I coordinated for the American Association for State and Local History (AASLH) 1997 annual meeting can assist a new director, or any director, to quickly assess in-

stitutional infrastructure and his or her suitability to strengthen it. See the AASLH technical leaflet, "New Director! New Directions?" by Anne W. Ackerson.

3. The New York statewide assessment and planning report, *Toward a Usable Past: Historical Records in the Empire State* (1984) was very useful in guiding and promoting great change over the next decade. While it set an ambitious agenda and recommended many strategies for addressing it, it did not try to provide detailed plans at that early stage. Later, other studies and reports could provide such detail on local government records, state government records, preservation, and other issues—after the groundwork was laid for action through more extensive analysis, grassroots consultation, a detailed plan of action, and coordinated advocacy.

4. See Larry J. Hackman, "With a Little Help from My Friends: External Advisory and Oversight Bodies in the Development of Archives," *Archivaria* 39 (Spring 1995): 184–195. This piece explores four examples of how external groups influenced and advocated important program development in New York. Sometimes relationships with influential individuals are best developed by exposing them to issues and needs as a member of an advisory group. They may then act both individually and as a member of the group on behalf of the archival program.

5. One excellent example is *Creating a Classroom for Democracy*, the case statement the Truman Library Institute developed for its very successful 1998–2000 capital campaign, which raised nearly $24 million. Another, aimed at informing a general audience about the importance of archives, was *Archives and You* produced by the New York State Archives. Guides and finding aids also represent an archival program, but they can't be expected to communicate effectively to audiences who don't already bring interest and understanding

6. Sometimes, an extended effort is needed to create a special revenue stream dedicated to archival purposes and to establish sufficient control over its use. New York examples include the creation of the Local Government Record Management Improvement Fund which required a major advocacy effort to authorize the state to collect some of the millions of dollars of records filing fees charged by local governments each year and to use these fees to support State Archives' technical assistance and grants to these local governments. A very different approach is represented by an agreement whereby funds would be transferred from state agencies each year to the New York State Archives which would then provide training and technical assistance to these agencies—but the agencies would be charged each year on the basis of their size, not on their use of the services of the State Archives. Hence the revenue stream was independent of the budget process and of the interest and priority that agencies gave to archives and records in a particular year. In some cases, an archival program may need to foster creation of a separate entity as a way to seek and control funds from sources outside the regular budget process. Examples include The New York State Archives Partnership Trust, a quasi-government entity created to enable the State Archives to seek private funding with the guidance and support of a powerful board of individuals representing both the private and public sectors. I plan to write soon about the role of the Truman Library Institute for National and International Affairs, the non-profit "partner" of the Harry S Truman Library.

7. The archives community would benefit from a curriculum and materials for education in program development, perhaps initially in the form of pilot workshops or an annual institute. There are few if any useful case studies that examine

closely the development of individual programs and no studies that evaluate program development methods on a comparative basis. For an early "mini-example,"
see Larry J. Hackman, James M. O'Toole, Liisa Fagerlund, and John Djoka, "Case
Studies in Archives Program Development," *American Archivist* 53 (Fall 1990):
548–560.

4

Strategic Approaches to Program Building in Government: From Local to International and Back

Liisa Fagerlund

BACKGROUND

The purpose of this chapter is to share reflections on my career history which has included positions in local and state government and in inter-governmental organizations. The chapter describes these experiences in sufficient detail to give readers an understanding of the background and environment as well as actions taken. It compares each situation in terms of a list of factors, such as top-level support and partnerships, which I have identified as being important to success and draws conclusions as to which elements are the most significant. Successful leadership must be based on solid professional standards and clear goals, preferably written, but the execution requires flexibility and adaptation for the current environment. The chapter is intended to give readers ideas for program development in their own settings.

Advancement for archivists usually requires mobility. Because archival programs are generally small and organizationally circumscribed, moving to a different, larger organization is often necessary to find new challenges and advance in the profession. My career history reflects this mobility. I have been fortunate to be able to take advantage of opportunities while indulging an interest in travel and new experiences.

The settings and major projects relevant to this chapter are as follows:

- Archivist, City of Portland, Oregon, 1977–1983: establishment of records management program, publication of records manual and archives guide;
- State Archivist, Utah State Archives, 1983–1986: change in program orientation from storage and microfilming to retention scheduling, reference, and information management;
- Records Management Officer, World Health Organization, Switzerland, 1987–1990: automating the registry inventory and extending service through a local area network;
- Information Officer, United Nations Advisory Committee for the Co-ordination of Information Systems, Switzerland, 1990–1992: planning for management of electronic records throughout the UN system;
- Chief of Archives and Records Management, United Nations, New York, 1992–1998: improving retention scheduling and implementing an electronic records management application to integrate electronic and paper records;
- City Recorder, City of Portland, Oregon, 1998–present: implementing an enterprise electronic records management application.

SUCCESS INDICATORS AND SUCCESS FACTORS

How do we determine that a program is successful? Here is a suggested list of positive indicators:

- Increased or reallocated funding—budget size and growth are the easiest measures, but reallocation of funding to better achieve professional goals can be equally important.
- Program outputs—visible products such as published guides, curriculum programs, grant awards, increased research use.
- Upgrading of staff—increased professional qualifications for staff and the resulting improvement in staff competency.
- Program development and growth—flourishing and institutionalization of program initiatives beyond grant periods and start-up phases.
- Professional recognition—awards from professional organizations and emulation of program elements by other agencies.

Table 4.1 indicates the presence or absence of each indicator in the various settings and gives my assessment of the degree of program success.

While success indicators identify program achievements, success factors are the primary ingredients—the conditions and actions that lead to a positive outcome. My suggested list of contributing factors:

- Recognized need for the creation of the program or for significant change in an established program. The recognition does not have to be universal, but key players have to be convinced of the need whether they are sponsors, staff, or professional colleagues.
- Top-level understanding and support. This comes naturally if the initiative originated with management or is gained through alignment with the goals and objectives of the sponsoring authority.

- Broad participation by staff so that they share the vision and are fully engaged in carrying out the work.
- Written plan of action providing vision, direction, goals, and activities to serve as a communication tool and as a benchmark for meeting goals and timetables.
- Guided by professional principles and standards.
- Effective partnerships—within the program and with other agencies.
- Opportunities to embrace innovation and engage in pioneering activities.

Table 4.1

Success Indicators	Portland	Utah	WHO	ACCIS	UN	Portland
Funding	Yes	Yes	No	No	Yes	Yes
Outputs	Yes	Yes	Yes	Yes	Yes	Yes
Staff upgrading	Yes	Yes	Yes	No	Yes	Yes
Program development	Yes	Yes	Yes	No	No	Yes
Professional recognition	Yes	Yes	Yes	Yes	No	Not yet
Overall success	Very	Very	Moderate	Moderate	Moderate	To be seen

Table 4.2 indicates whether or not these factors were significant in the case studies.

Table 4.2

Success Factors	Portland	Utah	WHO	ACCIS	UN	Portland
Recognized need	Yes	Yes	Yes	No	Yes	Yes
Top-level support	Yes	Yes	Yes	No	No	Yes
Staff participation	Yes/No	Yes	Yes	No	No	Yes
Written plan of action	Yes	Yes	No	Yes	Yes	Yes
Professional standards	Yes	Yes	Yes	Yes	Yes	Yes
Effective partnerships	No	Yes	Yes	Yes	No	Yes
Innovation and pioneering	Yes	Yes	Yes	Yes	Yes	Yes
Overall success	Very	Very	Moderate	Moderate	Moderate	To be seen

CASE STUDIES

City of Portland, Oregon, 1977–1983

The records management program for the City of Portland began under Stanley Parr in 1976 with a city-wide records inventory and development of a comprehensive retention schedule for city offices. Cost savings and increased efficiency were the justifications for improved records management, but finding funds to preserve historical records and make them accessible was more difficult. We requested funding from the National Historical Publications and Records Commission (NHPRC) to process the historical records, prepare computerized finding aids, and establish an archives program for the city. A three-year grant to establish the archives program as part of the NHPRC national inventory using SPINDEX software was awarded in 1978.[1]

The grant proposal served as a blueprint and a written plan of action for the archives program. It outlined the tasks to be carried out, specified methods and work standards, and included a timetable for completion, made rigorous because of the reporting requirements for the grant process. We knew that a guide to the archives had to be ready for publication by the end of the grant period and, to prepare the guide, all the records had to be described and entered into the computer system. This knowledge was always in our minds, keeping the project in focus and maintaining the momentum.

Inherent in the design of the program were professional standards and principles important to Parr as a historian and former staff member at the Texas State Archives and myself with a background of library and archival training and experience. Becoming involved in the national guide program of the NHPRC through the grant project and the use of SPINDEX meant that compatibility with developing standard practices in archival description was assured.[2] I was invited to give presentations on the Portland project at meetings of several professional associations, providing an opportunity for feedback and reinforcement from colleagues on the goals, methods, and activities of the project.[3]

An important element in the success of the program was the establishment of an automated system for archival finding aids. This was an early example of archival automation, utilizing a primitive form of word processing and a powerful but rigid mainframe application. *The City of Portland Archives Guide* was published in 1982 and served as a model for several programs in the Northwest.

The principal indicator of success in the Portland program has been the continued development and flourishing of the records management program: the institutionalization of retention scheduling procedures city-wide; the establishment and later expansion of an archives and records center; and growth of an important research collection for history of the city, its citizens, and its neighborhoods. The program has weathered budget-cutting cycles and has maintained a professional staffing level and commitment to professional standards of practice. Program outputs include the published guide, the comprehensive city retention schedule, and a rich database of administrative histories, series descriptions, listings and keyword indexing to the file folder level, accessible through a powerful retrieval system.

The support of management in the Auditor's Office was a major factor contributing to success in Portland. Top-level support from the City Council focused more on the cost-saving elements of the records management program than on the historical archives. Council supported the archival program largely because of the grant funding, and when authorizing the grant application the mayor wanted to be assured that we were not catering simply to "history buffs." As indicated earlier, the grant application provided an important written plan of action which had undergone professional scrutiny by NHPRC staff and peer reviewers. Being on the leading edge of archival automation gave the program credibility and effectiveness that helped to ensure its continuation and productivity. More recognized in national professional circles than in the local area, the initiative was initially viewed skeptically by established institutions like the Oregon State Archives and Oregon Historical Society. It took time for many city offices to gain confidence in its viability and effective partnerships were not to develop until later. Staff of the program was small and collegial which provided an environment where the critical follow through work needed to meet the grant project goals and complete the archives guide could be carried out.

Utah State Archives, 1983–1986

Utah State Government had participated in a massive effort to review its data processing and information management needs and capabilities and published the *Utah Systems Plan* in 1982. This initiative, headed by the governor, chartered a new, important role for the State Archives as the lead agency promoting openness and sharing of information in government records information systems while ensuring the protection of information about individuals.

When I began as the new state archivist in 1983, the archives program was strongly oriented towards microfilming and storage of records and ill prepared to take on this information management leadership role. My positive experience with performance planning for individual staff members in

Portland suggested that a planning process involving the entire staff would be an effective means of charting and implementing effective changes. With the guidance and enthusiastic participation of management of the Department of Administrative Services, the Archives' parent agency, a full-scale strategic planning process was conceived and underway within two months of my starting date.[4] Several success indicators and success factors are clear from the vantage point of over ten years later. The program already had a substantial annual budget so the indicator of success was not an increase in funding but a major reallocation of funding. A large budget for microfilm supplies and equipment was redirected to provide support for the upgrading of microfilm technician positions to professional records analysts and archivists. Some of the funding also went to tuition reimbursement programs to support those staff members in technical positions who wished to obtain professional qualifications and move into the new structure. Having the full support of management helped in this process. The director of Human Resources, the director of Finance, and I reported to the same, fully supportive, department manager. It is often difficult to reclassify positions and transfer funds between line items. But the administration sent a clear signal: the State Archives was moving in the right direction and every assistance was to be provided to the new director in what she and her colleagues were trying to do. The reorganization outlined in the Strategic Plan was given fast-track status by the Division of Human Resources. Within a few months, Lori Hefner and her staff of records analysts were producing a record number of retention schedules for review by the State Records Committee and a newly recruited head of reference, Jeff Johnson, opened a highly visible reading room for researchers at the state capitol.

According to the standards of archives and records management, the new state archives program was flourishing and it received considerable attention in professional circles for both its results and its methods. I was asked to speak to several professional organizations and to write a program description for the National Association of Government Archives and Records Administrators (NAGARA) *Clearinghouse* in addition to the *American Archivist* article referenced above.

As far as carrying out the information management leadership role envisioned by the *Utah Systems Plan*, program continuation is harder to measure. What was needed to fulfill the information management role was less clear than what was needed to carry out the archives and records management mission. We succeeded in developing a partnership with planning, library and information technology leaders, held a joint workshop on the management of electronic records, and participated in the development of a state government-wide data dictionary. In concept, this was an early government information locator system, but the difficulty of the software and the inability of archival staff to see how this related to the archives mission made interest in the initiative hard to sustain.

I consider the Utah experience to be very successful and to a large extent that experience serves as a benchmark for judging the other experiences. There was widespread recognition of the need for change and influential endorsement by departmental management reporting directly to the governor. It is hard to imagine more enthusiastic top-level support. This was especially valuable because of their support for the ideas, goals, and objectives of the professional archivists and records managers in the process.

World Health Organization, Switzerland, 1987–1990

The position of Records Management Officer for the World Health Organization (WHO) was an opportunity to live and work in Europe while being able to use English as my working language. The primary requirements for the post were experience with modern records and knowledge of computer applications.

Records management at the WHO meant the direction and supervision of the Registry, a centralized filing and correspondence management system which opened, classified, indexed, routed, and filed all substantive correspondence relating to the programs of WHO. A study conducted in the previous few years had advocated abolishing the Registry because of all the parallel filing systems maintained by departments. Staff throughout the organization opposed the recommendation on grounds that the Registry was vital as a safety net. Management determined that automating it would make it more useful and might reduce the need for duplicate departmental systems.

My mission was clear: use the emerging technology of the microcomputer to automate the Registry. But Registry staff members were skeptical about computerization because of an earlier failed attempt to produce an automated inventory of registry files and I needed to obtain their confidence. After studying the needs of the system and identifying the reasons for earlier failure, I consulted with information technology staff in the organization. They were promoting the use of standard, user-friendly, application-development software and were willing to provide assistance.

The automation of the Registry was a success. Involving Registry staff in the process, we were able to develop an inventory of Registry files with full text retrieval and reporting ability. We were able to print large labels for Registry files in a close approximation of the traditional format, produce sorted lists of Registry documents and ultimately provide access through

the newly developed Local Area Network. While the system did not immediately prevent the development and use of parallel departmental systems,
it provided a foundation for future development. Other success indicators
included the upgrading of staff through the recruitment of Louis Allegrini,
from another international organization, to fill a key position. Funding and
staffing for the program did not change, but during a time of cutbacks program level was maintained. Registry supervisors in Geneva requested
demonstrations and my paper on automation issues for registry systems
caused lively ongoing discussions at meetings of archivists/records managers of international organizations. The system continued to flourish and
grow in ensuing years, following my departure from WHO, another sign of
success. The original inventory of Registry files was expanded step by step
to the point of including the transmission of images of documents to Registry users, freeing departments from the need to maintain parallel files.

A number of success factors were in place at WHO. There was a clear
statement of direction by top management for computerization of the Registry and I ensured institutional support by the use of software selected by
the organization as a standard. There was some luck in the timing—the
new availability of user-friendly PCs and application development software for end users. A key factor was my determination to involve previously skeptical staff members in the design and redesign of the system. This
gave them ownership of the system as well as producing a more immediately useful product. Several staff members developed considerable expertise in formatting of the software and went on to design their own indexing
aids. Professional standards were maintained through the standardization
of names and indexing terms and the inclusion of disposition information.
The program was seen as an innovation for the organization due to the use
of PCs and the Local Area Network and benefited greatly from partnerships with staff of the library, information technology, and the office of the
new director-general.

United Nations, Geneva and New York, 1990–1998

My transfer from WHO to the secretariat of the United Nations Advisory
Committee for the Co-ordination of Information Systems (ACCIS) resulted
from my representing WHO on an ACCIS inter-agency technical panel on
electronic records. Archives, records, and information systems managers
from a number of organizations in the United Nations system formed the
membership, chaired by Richard Barry of the World Bank. The panel studied the use of electronic records in international organizations; the policies
and procedures for handling and maintaining electronic messages, docu-

ments and data; and problems, either current or anticipated. The landmark work, *The Management of Electronic Records*, drafted by David Bearman and revised by the panel was the result.[5] The report is frequently cited in discussion of electronic records and pioneered what later became well-established concepts such as "records as evidence of transactions" and "virtual archives."

Participating in the research and development of this report was an exciting and stimulating experience. An opportunity arose to join the secretariat of ACCIS and be involved with follow-up reports on technology standards relevant to the management of electronic records and curriculum materials for management briefings and implementation of the recommended programs. The position at ACCIS was attractive not only because it was a promotion but also because it would enable me to work on concrete methods for the management of electronic records. I served as Information Officer at ACCIS for two years, 1990 and 1991, and gained a sound theoretical knowledge of electronic records management issues and implementation guidelines.

Leading an actual implementation of these guidelines became possible in 1992 when I was appointed Chief of Archives and Records Management for the United Nations. My predecessor, Alf Erlandsson, who had been the United Nations representative on the technical panel before his retirement, had already begun the process by adding responsibility for the management of electronic records to the statutory mandate of the Archives and Records Management Service. However, when I began work, I found that there were other needs and priorities which had to be addressed before the issues of electronic records management could be pursued. The entire organization was in the throes of reorganization. The new Secretary-General, Butros Butros Ghali, had just taken office, the Assistant Secretary-General who had participated in my selection took early retirement, and I was reporting to a new manager who had not been involved in the efforts initiated by Erlandsson. We were receiving container loads of records from closed peacekeeping missions and we urgently needed to fumigate them, find adequate storage space, and develop retention schedules for mission records to prevent future problems. The system for describing and indexing archival records was inadequate and depended on experience and memory to provide reference service. The number of staff members was adequate, but the balance between clerical and professional staff was not. Another priority was replacement of the database software used for managing the records center.

Because of the success of formal planning processes in Portland and Utah, I intended to begin a strategic planning process. We needed to review the mission and objectives of the archives and records management program, consider the ACCIS guidelines for electronic records management, and develop an action plan to carry out the results. However, both in New York and in Geneva, I was in organizational areas that had not had favorable experiences with modern management techniques and top management was not supportive of this approach. I carried out an independent analysis of the situation and established projects to solve some immediate problems. To resolve problems with peacekeeping records, I visited the mission in Lebanon, inventoried records, and directed staff in developing a retention schedule for mission records. A six-month appointment of an experienced archivist produced a plan for revamping the archival processing, description, and finding aids system, including corporate name authority for frequently changing organizational names and programs. The budget process, combined with cost cutting and reform efforts, enabled us to reduce the number of clerical staff and move the salary savings to consultant funds which we used to contract with professional archivists for the processing of historical records. I had a mental action plan which, in retrospect, I would have done well to put in writing.

The need to meet the challenge of electronic records was also urgent. The ACCIS report, *Management of Electronic Records*, outlined a methodology for implementing an electronic records management program.[6] It was hard to see how the steps involving policy development and coordination could be followed without a formal planning approach. I learned that funds might be available from the information technology department to address an identified corporate priority: the replacement of the WANG mini-computer database in the records center. It was a logical step to incorporate electronic records issues in a consultant study to assess needs, recommend system requirements, and develop a request for proposal for the replacement hardware and software. In preparing background materials for the consultant, I included the ACCIS reports. Our meetings with departments confirmed the recommendations from the *Management of Electronic Records* for policies and practices concerning electronic records in all offices. When the consultant delivered the study report it included, in addition to hardware and software specifications, recommendations regarding electronic records management. The Archives and Records Management Service (ARMS) should obtain records management software capable of integrating the management of paper records in the archives and records repository with the management of electronic records from word processing, electronic mail, and other applications. The software selected to replace the records center database should also be used for a pilot implementation in ARMS and a selected secretariat office to establish a filing system for electronic documents, attach official retention schedules, and serve as an archival repository for electronic records.

The consultant's study became the written plan of action for the management of electronic records at the United Nations. An archivist experienced in information technology applications, Bridget Sisk, was selected to head the project. The RFP was issued, software selected and installed. The process of converting data from the minicomputer database was lengthy as were development of a filing plan and adaptation of existing and new retention schedules. However, we were successful in moving off of the minicomputer on schedule and carrying out storage, search, and retrieval activities for materials in the records center using the new software. The paper filing system for ARMS central files was loaded into the system and electronic documents and mail messages could be filed (or attached) to the same folder identification as for the paper records. We had achieved a functioning, integrated system.

At the same time as this was going on, we began developing clients, strategically located in the organization, for departmental pilot implementations for their electronic and paper records management. Successful projects would demonstrate usefulness, promote use in other departments, and lead to the adoption of the software as an enterprise solution for electronic records management.

The overall level of success in the United Nations experience was moderate. There were definite indicators of success: funding level was improved in spite of reform efforts and budget cuts, we were able to get new funding for the electronic records management system, and move money from clerical personnel to fund outsourcing of processing and description by professional archivists. We acquired and implemented records management software for integrated management of records in electronic and traditional formats. Where the experience fell short was in organizational support and in program development and growth.

The ACCIS report had made a strong case for electronic records management and the need was felt in departments at the working level as we found in our interviews with departmental staff during the consultant study. But management support was elusive. My immediate supervisor had a broad span of control, competing priorities, and was under fire in other areas of responsibility. Management of electronic records was not a mission he could adopt and actively promote and it was difficult to reach officials above his level. To sidestep this problem, I worked with technical staff outside of my organizational structure to promote the electronic records management project as an element in the development of standard technology products for the organization. Just as certain word processing, spreadsheet, and database software had been designated as organizational standards, we hoped to identify a standard records management application. To achieve this we included the information technology department, which had earlier funded our consultant study, in the preparation of the RFP, review of proposals, and selection of the software product. We considered them as partners in the project.

The success of the electronic records management initiative was limited. After my departure from the United Nations, a newly appointed information technology director, who had not been involved in the selection process, ordered that the use of the software be confined to ARMS and not extended to client departments such as the Office of the Secretary-General. Other aspects of the program are thriving, however, including the relocation to more convenient and modern facilities, so perhaps the broader outlook for success is more positive than is evident from the electronic records management experience.

The reliance on professional standards and their incorporation into concrete action plans, reports, and programs were critical success factors. The ACCIS report and consultant study were the most important, but also valuable was the blueprint on description standards and authority structure. The mission report that I wrote following my records management inventory of peace-keeping records in Lebanon was useful as a basis for developing records management procedures, general retention schedules, and mission records retention schedules. Partnerships were also important. In addition to involving information technology staff in the electronic records management project, we had great cooperation with records management counterparts in other international organizations, especially UNICEF. The sense that we were innovating and pioneering caused tension but also created excitement and motivation to succeed. When problems arose, we reminded ourselves that we were making history. It was satisfying to feel that we were actually filing and retrieving electronic records in an organized manner rather than just agonizing over the challenges they posed.

City of Portland, Oregon, 1998–present

The opportunity to work in the role of City Recorder attracted me to return to Portland after nearly 15 years away in Utah, Switzerland, and New York. To accomplish long-term accessibility of information, especially for electronic records, action is required at the beginning of the records life cycle, in the creation phase. That is what made my current job so inviting. As City Recorder I would supervise not only the archives and records management function, but also oversee the documentation of City Council proceedings and decisions. Staff of the City Recorder Division of the City Auditor's Office prepare council agendas, record proceedings, and assemble and maintain documentation of council decisions including ordinances, resolutions, reports, land use decisions, city code, and contracts. The City Recorder would be able to ensure that the indexing of council proceedings served archival needs as well as current retrieval by applying a standard thesaurus and making the index available to archivists and researchers. Just as I participated in the establishment of the archives and records center, now I would have an opportunity to promote the establishment of an electronic archives for the city.

It was gratifying to see on my return to city government that the archives and records management program was a strong and well-established part of city government. Early priorities for the City Recorder position included making the City Code available on the Internet and promoting the cleanup of the text and provisions since it would be more visible in searchable electronic form. A newly elected city auditor, Gary Blackmer, took office in 1999. He wished to gain a better understanding of the programs in his office and to find opportunities to improve processes and accessibility of information through wise use of information technology. He was receptive to participation in a strategic planning process, leading to the development of an information technology plan. He committed his time and that of his administrative deputy and the information system manager to participation in the process. The City Recorder division plus these three people engaged in a thorough planning process. We identified serious challenges faced by the city and determined that an enterprise records management system was the solution. It would upgrade and replace the software for cataloging the existing physical records, archive as many future records in electronic format as possible, and selectively convert past records. The City Auditor adopted the resulting "E-Files" project as his top priority. He campaigned with City Council members and influential directors for support and passage of his budget initiatives for the E-Files project. Funding was approved and planning is underway for selection, acquisition, installation, and configuration of the system in a two-year project.

It is too early to declare success, but there are a number of success factors in place. There is a recognized need for the project. Increasing reliance on information technology, awareness of problems of obsolescence and of the dangers of inadequate backup, as well as of inadequate deletion of electronic records, are in the news, and there are more products and techniques available to manage electronic records than there have been in my earlier experiences. The top-level support and leadership from an elected official is invaluable. He has the technological expertise to be an informed spokesperson for the project and his commitment to the importance of documentation of government activity and of citizen access to it is rock solid. There has been extensive staff participation in development of the project and on the project team. Written plans of action are integral to the process: the strategic plan report, the budget proposal, the request for proposal, and the project management document which will guide implementation. Professional standards are ensured both from participation by the archives and records professionals, Diana Banning, Jessica Hurley, and myself, as well as strong information technology representation. The team is committed to developing effective partnerships with user bureaus and technical advisors. From this vantage point, it appears that I will be able to see the development of a viable electronic archives for the City of Portland as a capstone project for my career.

CONCLUSIONS

This chapter offers ideas for successful program development, drawing on the variety of experiences in my career history. Case studies can pose difficulties in generalizing and applying lessons because of differences between the case study and one's own organization. Some of these differences include the scope and responsibilities of the archival program, the level of government, personalities and style of top management, size and strength of budgetary support, changes in the professional environment, and leadership qualities of the program director. In this chapter the same individual serves as the leader in each instance, controlling for one of the many variables. There are still too many variables for me to provide a roadmap for success, but my conclusions may offer some useful signposts.

To begin with, success is more likely if you choose positions where conditions are right for your preferred style of work. You need to define your own skills and motivating factors in managing your career development. Opportunities for change and innovation have been principle factors in my selection of new positions, in addition to the appeal of location. It has been important to me to be involved in projects that are on the leading edge and offer the opportunity to employ the best practices. I know that I prefer start-up phases and would rather build a program than maintain one that is already thriving. I also want to be sure that my participatory management style will be supported and that there is congruence between my goals and those of the sponsor. This is easier when you are recruited specially to be a change agent and work under the sponsor responsible for appointing you. I have left several positions, not because the job was finished or at a maintenance stage and I lost motivation, but because top management changed through elections or reorganizations, and the environment was no longer supportive.

When beginning a new assignment, it is helpful to talk to everyone, get their suggestions, and communicate your goals and ideas for change. I meet with each staff member, getting to know them, and seeking their perspective on positive and negative elements in the program. You get a lot of advice, often conflicting. One authoritarian-style peer manager told me that as a new director you have to bring in your changes in the first forty days. If you wait longer than that, people become complacent and harden their resistance to change. Another colleague, a trained organization development specialist, advised me that you should make no changes for six months while you studied the situation. Forty days is too soon to act, but it is important during the study period, however long it is, to signal to people in the organization that change is coming and to talk about your tentative findings as they emerge. People expect change when a new manager is appointed and are ready to accept it. If you wait too long, you will have lost your outsider status and your proposals may seem traitorous.

I resist pressures to immediately take on major responsibility for day-to-day activities of the program. It is essential to become familiar with policies, procedures, holdings, etc., but over involvement in operational demands interferes with the ability to see the big picture and identify innovative approaches. The leader's role is to plan but not to carry out all the work. In smaller programs involvement in day-to-day work may be unavoidable and the challenge will be to organize your time so that planning and leading is not squeezed out.

Flexibility is important in achieving success. Being skilled in management techniques such as strategic planning, business process re-engineering, quality analysis, etc. is helpful, but such techniques may not be applicable in a given situation. I wanted to employ strategic planning in all of my working environments, but met obstacles in the cultural climate of the international organizations in which I worked. Where that technique was embraced, in Utah and the City of Portland, it has been an important element of success. Progress is more assured when you use the techniques, processes, and methods that are approved or promoted in the organization. For example, at the WHO using the application development tool supported and promoted by the information technology department provided allies and helpers in making the project work.

Flexibility is required not only in the choice of management techniques, but also in how you present priorities. Identifying how the goals of your program fit with the priorities of your sponsor opens opportunities to turn your priorities into his or her priority. Having top level support is a won-

derful asset for a program. But sometimes that is difficult to get and you
have to be willing to try other approaches, such as the use of the technology
replacement project at the United Nations to promote electronic records
management. During the last year that I spent at the United Nations, an or-
ganization-wide reform initiative offered another avenue for the promotion of program goals. At the time I left, we were working to redefine the
electronic records management application as a reform project since it
would promote sharing of documents and save retrieval time.

In order for flexibility not to compromise quality and integrity, it is vital
to have a strong sense of where you are trying to go and what you want to
achieve. This sense is obtained by analyzing information gained in formal
review processes or personal observation and comparing the situation with
professional standards and state-of-the art trends. Since the profession is
developing so rapidly and change is constant, keeping up-to-date on research and experimentation must be routine. The director of libraries at a
large university once told me that managing the library system was just like
managing a sugar beet factory. I don't agree. Archival leaders have to have
sound theoretical knowledge and at least some practical experience to inform their vision and guide the direction of change.

Another important element has been the incorporation of goals and action planning in a written document. This has taken a different form depending on the environment. At the City of Portland it began with a grant
proposal, in Utah and later in Portland with a strategic plan report. Work at
the WHO was based on a previous study and official mandate; at the United
Nations on a consultant's study, internal reports, and the ACCIS report. Professional literature also provides sources such as self-evaluation instruments
provided by the Society of American Archivists and the National Association of Government Archives and Records Administrators. Having it in writing helps provide timetables and evaluation points; it also helps in
communicating goals and procedures to participants and sponsors.

Involvement of staff in all stages of planning and implementation of
change is an important key to success. You can't effectively delegate if direction is not communicated and priorities are not shared; and if you can't
delegate, your ability to achieve is limited. Group-planning processes are
the best way of engaging others in your goals and priorities and in developing a sense of shared vision, goals, and activities. Written plans are much
more valuable if staff members who have the principal role in making plans
a reality participate in the planning process.

The successful programs in which I have participated have involved
many other people who I can only begin to credit in a chapter of this length.
I hope the experiences I have described will encourage and stimulate youn-

ger archivists who are looking for direction in their careers and will cause other colleagues to reflect on what has worked for them as they faced the challenges of leadership.

NOTES

1. Originally developed at the Library of Congress, SPINDEX was database software written in Assembler language, employing typesetting mark-up coding to organize and index text and produce printed output.

2. The NHPRC was developing a national directory of archives and manuscript repositories including collection-level information.

3. Northwest Archivists Group, 1979, 1980; National Association of Government Archives and Records Administrators, 1980; SPINDEX Users Network, 1981; and the Society of American Archivists, 1981; essay in *Georgia Archive*, 1982.

4. Larry J. Hackman, James M. O'Toole, Liisa Fagerlund, and John Dojka, "Case Studies in Archives Program Development," *American Archivist* 53 (Fall 1990): 548–560, describes the planning process in detail.

5. *The Management of Electronic Records: Issues and Guidelines*, Geneva, ACCIS, 1990.

6. The methodology is summarized in my article on archives and electronic records at the United Nations in *ASIS Bulletin* 20, no.1 (October/November 1993): 19–20.

5

Strategic Planning and Implementation at the National Archives and Records Administration: 1992–2000

Michael J. Kurtz

INTRODUCTION

Over the past several decades, strategic planning has come to the fore in corporate America as one of the preeminent tools for charting strategic direction and exerting effective executive leadership. Though not without its critics, strategic planning is not only commonplace in the private sector, but also increasingly used in the public sector at the local, state, and federal levels. In fact, the Government Performance and Results Act of 1995 (GPRA) requires Federal agencies to develop strategic plans as a key element in achieving agency mission and improving performance.[1]

Strategic planning at the National Archives and Records Administration (NARA) actually predates passage of the GPRA by several years. Despite a relatively early start with strategic planning, NARA experienced a series of "false starts" and difficulties with implementation which eventually led to a new effort in 1995. All this reflected a complex organization undergoing a period of serious internal turmoil and buffeted by strong external factors. In other words, like many other organizations, NARA began its first experience with strategic planning in late 1992 with not a little hesitation and reluctance.

This chapter will focus on NARA's experience in developing and implementing strategic planning, with an emphasis on the current initiative which began in 1995. Nothing described is likely to cause the rewriting of management textbooks. But the lessons learned will hopefully prove of some assistance to other archival institutions caught up in the change management process.

ORGANIZATIONAL CONTEXT

In order to appreciate the NARA experience with strategic planning, it is critical to understand something of the organization's institutional framework and culture. The National Archives was originally established as an independent federal agency by an act of June 19, 1934. During the agency's first decade, the focus was exclusively on the archival mission—identifying, accessioning, preserving, and making available the historically valuable records of the federal government. Given the fact that the United States was the last industrial democracy to create a national archives, a tremendous workload ensued for the new agency.

The New Deal and World War II caused a tremendous explosion in the size of the federal government and created a flood of records requiring management and control. The National Archives, working with federal agencies and the military, began a records management program designed to assist agencies with the management and disposition of records. The Records Disposal Act of 1943 was a milestone in the creation of the government's records management program.

In 1949, as a result of government reform proposals resulting from the first Hoover Commission study, the National Archives was absorbed into the newly created General Services Administration (GSA) and became the National Archives and Records Services (NARS). This reflected the new dual, though complementary, aspects of the agency's mission.[2] Over the next 35 years NARS became a nationwide organization with a system of regional federal records centers and archives and a network of presidential libraries. NARS also retained the *Federal Register*, which was established and made part of the National Archives in 1936. When NARS once again became an independent agency in the executive branch on April 1, 1985—as the National Archives and Records Administration—its organizational culture was firmly in place.

The main characteristic of the culture reflected earlier organizational development and resulted in largely autonomous archival, records center, and presidential library systems with only general direction provided by central agency management. Though records management and records center functions had long been part of the agency's operations, the dominant ethos was archival and custodial in nature. Prior to the first strategic planning effort in 1992, managers responsible for major programs rarely functioned as a team. This, plus overlapping functions among the major program units, fostered a "stove pipe" mentality which made it difficult to deal with issues or problems that potentially confronted the agency (or the government). Another aspect of the "stove pipe" organizational structure was that most employees remained in their units during their careers. The lack of mobility within the organization reinforced the autonomous, narrowly focused aspects of the institution's culture.

Other aspects of organizational culture included a highly educated and trained professional workforce, with archivists and the archival mission setting the tone, for the most part, for the agency. As the dominant professional group, archivists shared a common academic background in American history and the experience of going through the agency's internal archival training program. Managers at the highest levels of the agency were almost exclusively products of the NARA system, spending their entire careers with the agency. Managers and staff from various professional backgrounds were knowledgeable and dedicated to the mission of the agency as perceived from the perspective of their program areas. By the time the first strategic planning effort began, the NARA had developed into the largest and most complex of any national archives, with extensive holdings and a nation-wide organization of almost 2,400 staff members.

THE FIRST STRATEGIC PLANNING EFFORT

Strong internal and external pressures forced the NARA to confront the need for systematic, agency-wide planning for the first time in its history. Prior planning efforts were focused around organizational components or for special projects, such as the building of a new archival facility in College Park, Maryland. By the fall of 1992, criticism from Congress and outside organizations about agency leadership and concerns about the NARA's performance of its mission led the Archivist, Don Wilson, to adopt a multi-point action plan. One important item was developing an agency strategic plan. The transition in the executive branch from one political party to another and a lawsuit focused on presidential electronic records served to complicate the strategic planning environment.

The archivist, with the assistance of a retired senior naval officer as a consultant, formed a management council of senior agency managers to work with him in developing the plan. In addition, a thirty-five member working group consisting of managers and staff from all the major organizational components of the agency performed the basic tasks of analysis and drafting the plan for management council review and approval. The strategic planning process took approximately three months, with a plan issued by the Archivist on February 23, 1993, shortly after he announced his resignation.[3]

What were the results and, perhaps most importantly, what lessons were learned? Leadership turmoil clearly mitigated the effectiveness of the process, the results, and the subsequent implementation. The management council, with no prior experience in working as a team and with no time provided for needed trust and team building, functioned poorly with little by-in from senior managers. The cumbersome working group reflected the turf-conscious concerns of agency units. Despite these caveats, there were positive elements in the process which laid the basis for further progress in the 1995 effort. The working group provided the first opportunity for many managers and staff to know and work with colleagues from other parts of the agency. The effort to identify and discuss issues from an agency—rather than program unit—perspective brought forth the first stirrings of an openness to change and experimentation. Numerous forums held for staff and for external interest groups provided not only opportunities for venting but also for new ideas and the articulation of expectations the agency was expected to meet. Though the management council had a rocky start, senior managers continued to meet as a group. Going back to earlier modes of operation was unthinkable and the basis was prepared for an evolution in executive leadership interaction.

The plan itself, subsequently modified in December 1993 and March 1995, did identify the major issues facing the agency—technology, inadequate resources, preservation, and the need for an effective records management program.[4] With an acting Archivist for twenty-six months lacking the legitimacy of presidential appointment and Senate confirmation and a deeply divided management council, effective across-the-board implementation of the strategic plan was not feasible. Yet, despite these problems some progress was made. Plans for organizational restructuring were developed that would bear fruit in the future. An effective equal employment opportunity program (EEO) was initiated, and implementation action in diverse areas such as records declassification, customer service standards, and privatization of certain order fulfillment services began.

THE 1995 INITIATIVE

In June 1995, John W. Carlin began his tenure as the eighth Archivist of the United States. As the former governor of Kansas and CEO of a high-tech company, Carlin had extensive experience in managing large organizations, operating in the public sector arena, and leveraging technology. In his first few months in office, the Archivist identified several strategic challenges confronting NARA. The explosive growth in office automation technology and electronic records presented major issues from the perspective of federal records management and traditional archival work processes. The agency needed a strategy to cope with new media formats at all points in the records life cycle from creation through disposition and possible archival use. Though NARA had developed a sound electronic records program, focused primarily on managing databases, additional expertise and a much-enhanced research and development effort were needed. Whether in the area of records creation, use, or disposition, new policies and expanded operational capabilities were required on an increasingly urgent basis.

The agency also faced a serious budget dilemma which threatened core operations and prevented the development of new initiatives. Over the course of many years, the NARA budget base had eroded as the agency had to absorb inflation, pay raises, and other personnel and administrative costs. With over thirty facilities around the country, many in rented space, the costs associated with space consumed almost 45 percent of the budget. Space costs were projected to rise to 60 percent within ten years. Personnel costs absorbed almost the entire portion which remained, leaving very little for research and development and other program needs.

Beyond the technology and budget issues, other factors concerned the Archivist. As a result of the turmoil of the previous several years, NARA was in management disarray. The agency was hampered by a lack of focus, leadership, and priorities. Further, the Archivist felt that the staff, though competent, dedicated to the agency's mission, and hard working, needed new skills to cope with a radically changed federal records environment and the resulting changes in archival work. He felt that an expanded range of skills in electronic records and records management were critical for future agency success. Not only did skills need to be enhanced, but the agency also had to make a systematic effort to recruit those with expertise and skills not already available with the on-board staff.

The Archivist soon ascertained that the strategic plan currently in place was not used to either "drive" the budget process or as a framework and catalyst for organizational change and transformation. Like any other newly installed executive, the Archivist needed to develop a vision to galvanize and redirect the organization. The Archivist decided that the best place to begin was to revamp the strategic planning process. He wanted to engage staff and constituents in a constructive dialogue on the agency's future. It was critical to build a shared commitment to a commonly held mission, vision, and values, and to determine priorities and set direction for the next ten years. As he confronted the long-term and immediate problems and obstacles, John Carlin was confident that a revitalized strategic planning process, along with consistent implementation over time, would result in dramatic progress for NARA.

STRATEGIC PLANNING PROCESS: THE FIRST STAGE

Though similar in certain respects, the new strategic planning process was fundamentally different from its predecessor. This effort began not only with the Archivist's commitment to the process, but with the forging of a top-level leadership team also committed to the process and to implementing the plan. Creating the team was a sensitive proposition. Senior NARA management had not heretofore functioned as a team working from an agency-wide perspective. Rather, the managers were responsible for their programs and reviewed issues from a generally limited perspective.

Using the services of an outside facilitator and consultant, the leadership team began a series of trust-building exercises designed to open up communication and understanding and build team unity. Other exercises focused on learning the principles of dialogue and inquiry as well as the steps involved in developing a strategic plan and understanding the requirements of the GPRA. Another key difference was that the Archivist and the leadership team developed a basic mission statement, vision, and set of values as the first step in developing the plan (see next section). While this was a collaborative effort, the Archivist did provide the working draft with his perspectives as a starting point for the discussion. This was a dramatic departure from prior experience. The earlier effort had a separate working group debate and draft various elements of the plan and then present them to the management council. This method of operation did not foster creative discussion or a sense of ownership. Another major difference involved a cross-section of NARA staff members working with the leadership team to fan out across the agency to gather input for developing the core of the plan. This Strategic Directions team, through a series of exercises, focused on team building and facilitation skills in order to conduct the agency-wide discussions.[5] Over a two-month period in the winter and spring of 1996 the team conducted open forums in all NARA facilities to solicit staff input on what steps should be taken to implement the vision and values laid out in the mission-vision-values statement. By the end of the process over 10,000 suggestions were proposed by more than one thousand NARA staff.

As the goals, objectives, and strategies began to take shape, input from external sources was also solicited. Getting interested individuals and outside groups involved in the process was critical not only to craft a good strategic plan but to get the critical "buy-in" needed to obtain support for implementing some of the more difficult and challenging goals. Initiatives in the electronic records and space arenas, for example, were bound to be both resource-intense and complex. The strategic planning process had thoroughly engaged the Archivist, the leadership team, NARA staff, and outside interest groups. Now, blessed by a plethora of recommendations, the task facing the Archivist and the leadership team was to craft an effective strategic plan to chart a new direction.

THE SECOND STAGE: A NEW DIRECTION

As previously noted, the Archivist issued a mission, vision, and values statement in August 1995, at the very beginning of the Strategic Directions Initiative. This provided the framework for the first part of the strategic planning process, the analysis and input phase. But the mission, vision, and values were critical for the second phase of the strategic planning process, when the plan was crafted and an intense period of review, debate, and discussion ensued. The mission statement committed NARA to ensure ready access to essential evidence for all citizens. The underlying vision was that the National Archives "is a public trust on which our democracy depends." NARA's role was to ensure "continuing access to essential evidence" in federal and presidential records which document "the rights of American citizens, the actions of federal officials, and the national experience."[6]

NARA's responsibility encompasses all federal records at each stage of the records life cycle, not just at the archival stage. Records could contain essential evidence documenting the rights of citizens, accountability of public officials, and the national experience, for certain periods of time and not others, with some records having a continuing value requiring extended preservation and access. The fundamental thrust was to broaden the agency's perspective beyond the archival and custodial. It should focus in an intense manner on the need for access to essential evidence contained in records at all stages of the life cycle, whether or not destined for archival retention, and regardless of where such essential evidence is found or where users are, for as long as needed. This was an activist stance designed to revitalize NARA's and ultimately the government's records management role. The mission and vision were complemented with a set of values the Archivist identified as critical for mission and agency success. From the Archivist's perspective, all employees had to value risk-taking, communication, commitment, and loyalty if the agency had any hope of achieving an ambitious ten-year vision.

Once the mission, vision, and values component was in place, Archivist Carlin launched the overall Strategic Directions initiative in August 1995 with a statement to all NARA staff defining the key concepts for agency planning. This message was reinforced in a nationwide video presentation by the Archivist for NARA staff; by printing the mission-vision-values statement on posters as a visible reminder to all staff; and by creating an electronic suggestion box for comments and suggestions. As previously noted, the Strategic Directions team followed up with brainstorming sessions at all NARA facilities collecting numerous proposals, suggestions, and concerns. By early April of 1996, the Archivist and the leadership team confronted the task of crafting the goals and strategies required to turn challenges into opportunities.

Besides staff input, there were numerous other sources for additional input into the plan. These included a review of NARA's statutory and legislative authority and mandates, previous strategic plans and reports, staff and customer surveys, and discussions with key constituents—all in all a plethora of data. Now was the time for focus and purpose.

Key environmental factors shaped the development of the four general strategic goals designed to achieve the mission and vision. The key factors were the varied needs of NARA's users and the variety of constituents requiring services from the agency. Further, the continuing explosion of paper records, an unexpected byproduct of the electronic records revolution, along with the impact of technology on recordkeeping, all required new, innovative approaches.

Built around the key mission statement, "ready access to essential evidence," the four goals drafted by the Archivist and his team were:[7]

1. Essential evidence will be created, identified, appropriately scheduled, and managed for as long as needed.
2. Essential evidence will be easy to access regardless of where it is or where users are for as long as needed.
3. All records will be preserved in appropriate space.
4. NARA's capabilities for making changes necessary to realize our vision will continuously expand.

Each goal was further refined with a set of specific strategies and the identification of key performance targets and measures. All were pegged to the ten-year vision forming the framework for the entire strategic plan. The performance targets and measures were designed to not only put teeth into the implementation but also to link performance, mission, and resources as required by the GPRA. The specific strategies and performance measures were a bold attempt to shift agency culture and operations to meet electronic records demands, space needs, and customer requirement from problems to opportunities for growth and a new direction.

After the draft plan was completed in July 1996, comments were sought from NARA staff and the public. Two lengthy sessions with NARA stakeholders, customers, and interest groups took place. Participants provided critical comments and suggestions designed to stimulate a more outward-looking and activist agenda. The Archivist issued a nation-wide video to the staff describing the plan and seeking comments. The plan was sent to key constituent groups and put on the NARA website, and the Archivist sent various columns to constituent newsletters. In a further effort to stimulate interest and feedback, the Archivist held open forums for federal agency officials, congressional staff members, historians and genealogists, archivists and records managers, educators, and veterans' representatives. All in all, NARA carried out a determined effort to internal and external "buy-in," critical for the important implementing phase.

IMPLEMENTING "READY ACCESS TO ESSENTIAL EVIDENCE"

After further refinement of the plan to meet all requirements of the GPRA, the strategic plan was issued by the Archivist on September 30, 1997. The next step was developing an annual agency performance needed to turn vision into reality. There were six areas identified for initial progress on implementation.

First, and perhaps most critical, staffing and budget priorities were realigned to reflect the goals, strategies, and performance measures of the strategic plan. Staff assignments, recruiting new staff, and budget allocations and submissions all began to reflect the agency focus on records management, electronic records, and preservation. While not denying the need for the traditional custodial tasks performed by the agency, budget and staffing changes reflected a commitment to reinvigorate federal management and NARA's role in that arena. Electronic records and preservation, particularly for non-textual media, were areas also affected by redefined staffing and budgetary priorities.

Another critical step was developing the infrastructure needed to bring the plan to life. With the records life cycle as the animating concept in the strategic plan, the logical next step in the implementation was to reorganize agency operations around the life cycle work processes. Early in 1997, two integrated life cycle records services units were established. Both units, one for the Washington, D.C. area and the other for field operations, combined records management, archival, and public programs activities into a unified organizational structure. Units with overlapping functions and responsibilities were merged, dramatically cutting back on coordination and "turf" issues and enabling resources to be better utilized in tackling large issues and problems emphasized in the strategic plan such as records management, improved working relations with federal agencies, and electronic records. [8] Led by the Archivist, a series of agency dialogues with federal agencies took place resulting in, among other things, the creation of targeted assistance staff positions designed to work with agencies to address records management problems faced by agencies.

Access to records and information was the hallmark of the strategic plan's vision. Yet, significant portions of NARA's archival holdings were restricted because of continued national security classification. A major initiative during the early implementation of the plan was a vigorous agency effort to declassify records pursuant to President Clinton's Executive Order 12958. Within the first year of the Order (1995–1996), NARA was leading the government in pages declassified and in providing major assistance to agencies in their declassification efforts. A veritable flood of previously withheld documentation became available to researchers.

The final area, though perhaps the most critical for the agency's long-term viability, was the development of a major electronic records project. With increased funding from Congress provided because of the imperatives presented in the strategic plan and in budget presentations by the Archivist, NARA was able to develop a research and development partnership with other federal agencies and with the San Diego Supercomputer Center. The project, still ongoing, is designing an electronic records archive to manage the life cycle of electronic records. The project has major significance for federal records management as well as archival access to electronic records. Without a successful project, NARA faces very limited prospects for providing "ready access to essential records" in the electronic arena. A successful project, the result of a clear strategic vision, helps ensure a vital institution.

A ten-year strategic plan is not realized in a day, month, or year. Evolution and continued implementation are the hallmark of a vital plan. Though NARA began vigorously in implementing its strategic plan, obviously much remains to be accomplished.

WHAT IS LEFT?

The most difficult challenge facing NARA in implementing its plan is the issue of transforming the organizational culture. Though reordering priorities, reorganizing operations, and creating innovative new strategies are complex and challenging, the issue of changing how the staff and institution think, approach problems, and relate are the most difficult aspects of

changing attitudes

implementing a strategic vision. Assisting managers and staff in developing new approaches to problem solving and group dynamics is a slow and often painful task. The agency's leadership must take the lead as role models and ensure the development of a new human resources infrastructure designed to foster a new organizational culture.

Key elements include creating individual development plans for employees to assist in developing new skills and in furthering agency objectives and individual career goals. Further, as part of implementing the strategic plan, the agency intends to create a new performance management system tying individual performance to GPRA goals and creating a new, more flexible environment conducive to experimental work teams and other innovations. Buttressing all this is an agency-wide training initiative focused on job skills, interpersonal skills and relationships, professional development, and valuing workplace diversity. Cynicism about "fads of the day" is difficult to overcome and requires persistence over time to show true agency commitment to the values enunciated in the strategic plan. It is fair to note that the greatest challenge for NARA's strategic plan lies ahead—creating a new organizational culture.

CONCLUDING OBSERVATIONS

Though the efficacy of strategic planning is often disputed in professional circles, there is no debate about the need for an engaged chief executive officer (CEO) in providing direction and leading change. The single greatest difference between NARA's current plan and its predecessors is the commitment and involvement of the Archivist in leading the effort. Top-level commitment and continuity through the first years of implementation provided the needed momentum to move forward. The point is that the boss must be committed, involved, with a stable position. Nothing can compensate if these factors are not present.

The organization's senior leaders need to be fully engaged and committed to achieving the strategic vision, for it is on their shoulders that much of the implementation will fall. Team building and skill enhancement is even more critical for this group than others further down in the organization. Most critically, the senior managers must function as a team tasked with achieving the vision throughout the organization, and not merely as executives of their particular department. Overall, it is fair to state that an effective strategic planning process and implementation requires a tremendous amount of time, effort, and commitment at all levels of the organization. It truly has to become, for a period of time, the focus of the entire organization.

The basic process followed by NARA reflected the accepted norms in a strategic planning initiative. Environmental scans, data gathering and analysis, setting out the mission, vision, and "business" of the organization, along with goals and objectives, were all elements of a systematic planning effort. Getting genuine staff and external input at various stages along the process is critical. For at the end of the process the real work begins. Support is critical from a funding and programmatic perspective. Without support and enthusiastic "buy-in" little will be achieved.

The impact of this strategic plan has been significant, if not profound. In the records management and electronic records arenas, major initiatives are addressing long-standing problems and urgent realities. A strategy for the long-term preservation of non-textual records, with additional funding from Congress, addresses a major threat to archival memory. The plan and subsequent implementation has attempted to focus on issues critical to the agency's future. The verdict on ultimate success is still in the future but the leadership provided and process followed have resulted in a focused burst of creative energy.

Without a strategic plan NARA, like any other organization, will be constantly consumed with current problems and issues and no framework for tackling medium and long-term threats and opportunities. Public institutions are particularly susceptible to a short-term "crisis" perspective as constituent and oversight groups push their agendas. A strategic plan doesn't guarantee success, but the lack of one is a serious detriment.

The essence of NARA's strategic planning experience is applicable, I believe, to smaller or less complex programs and organizations. Leadership, teamwork, mission focus, goals, and objectives are applicable in any setting. A clear sense of the "business," threats and opportunities, and a roadmap to where the program needs to go are all needed for any successful program. A strategic plan can be simple or complex; it is the quality of the thought that goes into the effort which can make the difference between success and failure.

Certainly for NARA the strategic plan has provided a focused and effective way in explaining the agency's mission, value to society, and the challenges facing the institution. This has enabled the agency to interact with Congress and our constituents in a clearer and more organized manner, resulting in a much higher degree of financial and program support. A strategic plan is not a panacea or guarantee of success. But NARA can certainly demonstrate the benefits of undertaking the effort. In a technologically and societally complex world, there is no substitute for effective strategic planning. Without a good plan, effectively implemented, the potential for success is greatly reduced.

NOTES

1. Management trends in corporate America are always a bit delayed in coming to the fore in the public sector. The management literature on strategic planning reflects this fact. Collections of essays such as *The Strategic Management Handbook* (New York: McGraw-Hill, 1983) edited by Kenneth J. Albert and *Readings on Strategic Management* (Cambridge: Ballinger, 1984) edited by Arnoldo Hax reflect the near total sweep of strategic planning in the corporate world in the 1980s. However, Henry Mintzberg's *The Rise and Fall of Strategic Planning* (Toronto: The Free Press, 1994) critiques strategic planning and management and expresses deep skepticism about the value of a top-down strategic planning system.

2. The only published work on the history of the National Archives is Donald R. McCoy's *The National Archives: America's Ministry of Documents, 1934–1968* (Chapel Hill: The University of North Carolina Press, 1978).

3. *The National Archives and Records Administration: Strategic Plan for a Challenging Federal Environment, 1993–2001* (Washington, DC: National Archives and Records Administration, 23 February 1993).

4. Updates to the basic strategic plan adopted in February 1993 were issued in December 1993 and March 1995.

5. Memorandum (NARA96–029) "Strategic Initiatives Update, 8 November 1995," Record Group 64, Records of the National Archives and Records Administration, College Park, Maryland.

6. *Ready Access to Essential Evidence: The Strategic Plan of the National Archives and Records Administration, 1997–2007* (Washington, DC: The National Archives and Records Administration, 30 September 1997), p.5.

7. *Ibid.*

8. Memorandum (NARA98–098) "Next Steps on Strategic Plan Implementation, 11 February 1998," Records of the National Archives and Records Administration, Record Group 64.

6

Corporate Culture and the Archives

Philip F. Mooney

THE ROLE OF ARCHIVES IN BUSINESS

All organizations, regardless of their financial base, establish operational frameworks that dictate the daily pace of institutional life. Traditional archival programs measure their success on the quality of scholarly research conducted with their collections. To that end, the development of detailed descriptive finding aids and an emphasis on solid reference service characterize quality performance standards in the field. Conversely, the business community views history from a more pragmatic perspective. The value of history is calculated against the contribution it makes to the corporation, and the archivist must manage programs and allocate resources against that philosophical background. To function effectively in either environment, the professional archivist must understand the cultural patterns and values of the institution and create programming that supports and enhances them.

In the academic community, the rules and roles are generally well defined. Colleges, universities, and historical societies understand and embrace the development of strong documentary collections that will support advanced research projects. They respect and appreciate archival functions and clearly recognize them as compatible with the charter of the parent organization. Financial support and resource allocation for the archives cer-

tainly are dependent on the economic well-being of the institution and its
stated priorities, but there is a shared vision. By contrast, in the business
community there is an inherent contradiction between the futuristic corporate mission statement and the perceived archival focus on preserving the
past. The contemporary corporation values innovation, creativity, and
risk-taking in bringing products to market—qualities that seem antithetical
to standard archival practice. How, then can an archival program exist and
even thrive in such a seemingly hostile environment?

Over 250 corporations in the United States value their heritage enough
to support an archival program though their rationales and structures for
doing so may vary widely. In some cases, the archival work is combined
with another function that manages information or handles records. Corporate libraries and information centers populate many business organizations because of their ability to provide quality technical, legal, and
marketing information to their clients in a cost-effective fashion. Information specialists understand the nature of research and the wide range of resources that can be explored to secure data that will enable departments
and associates to meet their objectives. Since archivists and librarians share
similar skill-sets, it is not uncommon to see the groups linked in either a direct or indirect fashion. Librarians serving as archivists, archivists reporting to librarians, or separate departments reporting to a common point are
models frequently seen on organization charts.

Similarly, since records management programs monitor the life cycle of
records from creation to destruction, some businesses will consider the
management of records with a permanent retention classification to be a
natural extension of the records manager's responsibilities. The archivist-
records manager can provide a "one-stop shopping" solution to all issues
relating to records generated by the corporation. Still other organizations
separate records that have permanent historical value from the large volume of records that move through a corporation and establish an independent archival unit to care for them. In these situations, the clear message
is that the corporation has formally recognized the relevance of history to
the business. The job of the archivist is to make sure that it remains relevant
over the long term.

Regardless of the structure that surrounds them, the most common de-
nominator in the existence of corporate archival programs is their ability
to provide customized, relevant information to the business that would be
difficult and expensive to secure from third-party vendors. Such services
become even more important in highly-competitive industries where
"speed to market" is imperative and confidentiality is critical in the development and marketing of products and services. One way to think about cor-

porate archival programs is to view them as in-house consultancies that manage resources in support of the corporation's goals and objectives. The closer that archival work parallels the ideas and concepts embodied in such documents, the more relevant it will become and the more resources it will receive.

While departmental charters, annual business plans, regular management reviews, and monthly or quarterly reports are useful tools for any archives, they are essential elements for the corporate archivist. They provide a formal mechanism that outlines the specific duties of the department, provides concrete evaluation tools that measure success or failure, and creates a dialogue that allows the archives to grow with the parent body. No archival program can exist in a vacuum, but the level of two-way interaction must be elevated in a corporate setting. A consistent, regular, focused communications strategy with various levels of management allows for feedback on departmental operations and can provide insight to current thinking on the executive level.

In an age when managers regularly receive updated information on emerging business issues, concise voicemail messages and well-crafted e-mail documents on departmental projects can help position the archives as an integral part of the operating structure. The use of web-based technologies to gain presence on Internet/intranet sites helps to raise awareness of an archival presence and allows opportunities for both positive and negative commentary on content. Frequently, archivists discover documents in their collections that may have relevance to issues of current importance to management. The circulation of such documents with an appropriate message underscores the value of an internal history department that can provide useful case studies on previous "best practices." Above all, regularly scheduled meetings with management to review progress against objectives ensure that the activities of the department are consistent with corporate priorities. As shifts in policies and philosophies mandate changes in organizational structure and activities, the archival work must adjust to a fluid environment. To remain uninvolved and unengaged with management is to invite disaster.

One excellent method of soliciting an exchange of ideas is through the creation of a "Destination Document" that outlines where the program is going and what the desired results will be. Rather than focusing on past achievements, it takes a more futuristic approach to the results that management can expect to see from an allocation of resources. For the archivist, such a document can place proper emphasis on a "return on investment" and can make strategic thinking a paramount part of work plans, annual reviews, and budget submissions. While data on research requests, reference questions answered, and collections processed are meaningful to compile and demonstrate levels of activity, there must be business-related results to generate long-term support in terms of both personnel and finances. "Destination Documents," at all levels of the organizational structure, are innovative and active charters that grow, change, and adapt to business conditions in a world where communications and technology advances change the landscape regularly. An archives that understands these realities and that can frame its activities accordingly will become an important and respected partner on the road to a shared vision.

A good "Destination Document" should parallel the characteristics of personal performance programs that many individuals adopt to measure growth and development. It should project both short- and long-term objectives for the department, showing clear links between resources and results. It should also include a projection of quantifiable results that allows the project to be properly evaluated. For example, one shared objective might be to convert a standard photographic collection to a digital library available at the desktop of all associates globally. To achieve this destination will require an allocation of resources for scanning, technical support, hardware and software, and possibly additional personnel. The desired result will be an interactive information system that allows associates to retrieve images at their convenience to apply against current business projects. The usefulness of such a tool can be measured against the "hits" it receives and qualitatively against the importance of the initiatives it supports. Extending this concept to the range of archival activities provides management with a series of checkpoints to weigh the value of such projects against other programs competing for dollars.

While business units engaged in direct sales activities generate profits that go directly to the bottom line, many corporate functions represent "overhead" costs that must be cost-justified to both management and shareowners. Public relations, community affairs, consumer relations, corporate services, and even advertising and marketing are not revenue-generators, but over time, they have gained acceptance in corporate America because they generate positive publicity, foster strong community ties, respond to consumer inquiries, provide essential internal services, or create the tools that allow the business to sell its services. Benchmarking against such functions, the archives needs to emphasize the value of the unique information it manages. Without historical documentation, books, articles, news stories, and documentaries would not exist, and the equity of the firms' trademarks, slogans, patents, packaging, and promotional activities would be compromised. In reporting on activities and projects, the emphasis should focus on the business benefit received.

Just as the corporate archivist must think like business associates in developing long-term plans for the organizational unit, there are other examples of modeling that should be followed. Positions and job grades in the department should be parallel to other managerial roles that entail responsibilities for knowledge management, resource allocation, and interface with internal and external audiences. These comparisons should not be solely against library and records management functions, but against entire classes of management that have similar responsibilities, such as marketing, public relations, learning consortia, and human resources. The wider the base of comparison, the more elevated the job grades and pay scales become for the archivist.

The standard evaluative tools used to grade corporate positions focus on credentials, interface with management, the value of resources managed, and the number of people directly influenced by the job. Most archivists easily qualify on the credentials issue with their academic degrees and training, but the other components can prove more difficult to document. For this reason alone, networking becomes an unstated but critical job skill for corporate archivists. By understanding the nature of work in the marketing, public relations, legal, and human resources areas, the archivist can craft programs and develop informational vehicles that foster mutual interdependence. These initiatives expand the role of the archives and its sphere of influence and can require a revisitation of the archivist's job responsibilities. As the resources of the collection are applied against the ongoing business, the value and importance of the archives is positively affected.

Even the job title itself can help to communicate the positioning of the archives to the work population. Terms like "manager," "director," and "vice president" establish a clear hierarchy of rank, but the "archivist" designation has no meaning and consequently little respect. To be considered an equal, the archivist must adapt to the trappings of the environment and lobby for a position description and titles that are comparable across the organization. Such a positioning will establish a broader frame of reference in determining job grades, compensation levels, incentive payments, and stock options.

Similarly, whenever possible, the archives should occupy a physical location that is part of the headquarters complex in a location that is visible to the workforce. Remote locations, consignment to a basement area, or other forms of separation can signal a view of the function that associates readily receive. An archival program that is integrated with other business functions operates from a position of equality and respect. Public relations, community affairs and related departments must have access to their clients to perform their job responsibilities effectively. Nobody would ever consider consigning these groups to remote locations where they would be isolated from their users. Archivists require the same level of interaction to fulfill their mission and to meet management expectations. Additionally, if the Archives is separated from the main campus, it will lose credibility and presence as a vital element in the corporate infrastructure. The resulting effects can be devastating. If the department is "out-of-sight," it is "out-of-mind."

In all large organizations, reporting relationships determine the quality and magnitude of distributed resources. Departments close to the top of the pyramid receive both attention and support, while those groups closer to the base will compete for remnants. Archives in corporate settings generally occupy these lower tiers because their functions are not easily classified into typical job groups. Without an obvious placement, they tend to drift into foster homes that tolerate their presence and offer them a temporary safe harbor. Most frequently, public relations, administration, legal and the office of the corporate secretary serve as homes to business archives. Depending on the nature of the organization, such positionings can be either positive or negative.

The key factor is access to decision-makers, who can, in turn, influence the flow of resources to the archives. While organizations differ radically in their structure, the archives requires a direct link to the higher echelons of management. Because all such placements are inherently unnatural, the archivist has both a challenge and an opportunity. The challenge is to structure the archival functions in ways that are meaningful to business people. The opportunity lies in the fact that, regardless of the initial placement, an aggressive archivist can work to find a more responsive, supportive environment with minimal political repercussions. In most corporations, management of the archives is not a core business unit that has a natural link to a particular department. Consequently, if the archivist identifies a better placement opportunity and can develop sound arguments for the change, management often will acquiesce.

CREATING A RELEVANT BUSINESS PLAN

Just as corporate objectives must change to meet new business opportunities, the corporate archivist must develop goals and objectives that are flexible and consistent with a rapidly evolving marketplace. Annual business plans typically include projections on sales increases, revenue growth, and increases in market share. Archival initiatives should adopt similar approaches to work output by establishing a series of measurable objectives that business people can understand and evaluate. The development of an intranet heritage-based website, the processing of a specific number of collections, the creation of a set of pamphlets and brochures, the development of an orientation presentation for new hires, the design and fabrication of a set of traveling exhibits, or the conversion of an audio-visual collection to digital formats are all examples of initiatives that management can evaluate in terms of the time and resources expended against them versus the utility and impact of the finished products. Using a disciplined analytical approach to departmental activities, purpose-driven work will replace activity-based work and render more relevant service to the organization.

Archivists spend much of their time looking at tasks and processes rather than concentrating on the larger question of mission. The daily pressures for immediate answers often impede the organization from realizing higher levels of achievement that would create stronger links to key constituents. A focused approach to work assignments coupled with the organization's "Destination Document" helps to set those priorities that yield business-focused results.

Most business units prioritize their efforts against activities that produce results that management recognizes and rewards. They ignore distractions that may impede them from reaching their goals even when other requests for services are legitimate. A public relations professional will spend hours working with *Fortune* magazine when a profile of the chairman of the board is being written. If other requests for information happen to occur in the same time frame, they may or may not get answered because a clear hierarchy of need has been established. On the other hand, many archivists try to handle information flow without the same level of discernment or focus. The inevitable result of such an approach is a diluted work product that may appear trivial to administrators making critical assessments of departments and functions. To succeed in business, the archivist must think like a businessperson and manage strategically.

One of the primary reasons to jointly develop destination documents, departmental charters, and annual business plans is to establish criteria for success. They should provide solid outlines of the results that are expected over one-, three-, and five-year cycles. They will also identify the measurement criteria that will be employed in the evaluative process, and they will impose a discipline on work that will drive activities on a weekly and monthly basis. In setting priorities and establishing workflow, they serve as a critical measuring stick in determining appropriate levels of activity.

From a purely archival perspective, working with corporate records offers limitless opportunities. The sheer volume of material in multiple formats generated by a contemporary business offers a lifetime of possibilities for archivists seeking to preserve its documentary heritage. Even with the most scrupulous appraisal procedures, the quantity of material is stagger-ing, and therein lies the problem. Faced with a continuous flow of docu-mentation, business archivists can easily fall victim to a forest fire mentality that results in a failure to become more integrated with the business and re-sults in missed marketing opportunities.

Mission statements and destination documents can help structure goals and objectives, but only if they are living documents that will change and evolve with the corporation. Too often such documents become stone tab-lets that are periodically dusted off and reissued without ever asking a key series of questions: Is the work we are doing the right work? Could we be doing it better? Can we do it differently? Should we be doing other things? Is what we are doing relevant to the business?

In order to answer these questions, the archivist needs to poll the cus-tomers and clients who use departmental services. Analyzing stakeholders and their requirements for information will often reveal hidden levels of expectation as well as unexplored opportunities. In developing mecha-nisms to receive feedback, start with the "frequent shoppers." Those de-partments and groups that use archival resources in their work have already recognized the value of historical data and have become depend-ent on the availability of the information supplied. With proper handling, such groups can become strong internal advocates, but they must be culti-vated and respected.

Whether formally or informally, quality and speed of service should be reviewed. Was the information accurate and complete? Was it delivered in a timely fashion? How could the service be improved? What activities or work products should the archives provide that it is not currently doing? The answers received to these questions help managers assess the strengths and weaknesses of the program and offer an independent view of the func-tion. Listening carefully and incorporating the learnings from these ses-sions will move the archives closer to the mainstream of the business and will stimulate the development of revised work charters more grounded in reality.

Once the low-hanging fruit has been harvested, the archivist can begin to examine areas of the business where history is not an active concern. De-partments that seldom or never use the archives may not do so simply be-cause they were unaware of the collection or its potential usefulness to their work. In these cases, the archivist must take the initiative to demonstrate relevance and to suggest possible historical applications to current projects. For many consumer goods companies, the marketing of their products and services spans decades, but the basic components and selling messages for those programs has remained consistent. It is very possible that a newly minted MBA could learn valuable lessons from a review of previous campaigns if somebody brought the information forward. Many corporations look to share "best practices" through interactive CDs, printed case studies, and shared databases. The historical perspective should be represented in all of these tools. It is unlikely that any corporate program will secure universal acceptance, but every new user broadens the clientele.

Such self-examinations are not one-time processes. They need to become a regular element in aligning the archival mission with that of the parent body. In creating this ongoing system of receiving feedback from multiple sources, the archives will develop a stronger internal support system that will validate its value and endorse its services. By cultivating a broad spectrum of users and customizing services to meet specific organizational needs, the archives assumes a pro-active leadership role by re-purposing historical assets for contemporary applications.

THE ARCHIVAL FUNCTIONS REVISITED: A PRACTICAL VIEW OF ARCHIVAL WORK

While the traditional archival functions of reference, access, arrangement, and description exist in the corporate environment, the nature of the work differs radically from the practices of academic counterparts. The philosophical underpinnings of corporate archives run contrary to the operating principles of public, non-profit, and university-based repositories. A corporate archives, more properly considered as a company resource rather than a research facility, takes a very insular view of its holdings and directs its energies towards its internal clientele, and applies the archival functions accordingly.

With the exception of a publications project, an audio-visual production or some form of pre-approved academic study, the staff, on behalf of internal clients, conduct virtually all of the research projects that flow into the department. Because the nature of corporate records contains extensive proprietary information that, if released, could negatively impact the business, most programs do not permit external research in their collections. The entire rationale for creating and maintaining an archives is to serve the informational needs of the parent institution. Since the archives consists of records created and funded by a private entity, no obligation exists to open materials to public scrutiny. In fact, the litigious nature of American society and concerns over negative publicity mandate that extreme caution should govern the release of even the most benign documents. Moreover, opening collections to outside researchers would divert staff time and energy from handling internal requests and expanding internal capabilities. In large part, the archivist-researcher determines the legacy of the corporation through the use of records, the issuance of reports, and the types of documents used to create authorized histories. These interpretations become the corporate memory and create the cultural values that shape the decision-making processes.

The inherent challenge in this model is to manage the research to the greatest benefit of the department and to the parent institution. All research requests do not merit the same level of attention just as all business units do not receive the same levels of exposure and support. Archivists must establish a hierarchy of response that is linked to results and recognition. High visibility projects, where the archival component is clearly identified, get clear priority over the more mundane requests that can occupy similar time commitments with none of the tangible rewards. The "big bang" approach to research becomes a cornerstone of practice.

Arrangement, description and appraisal also vary from standards that govern activities in the non-profit and governmental sectors. Because the research function is internalized, the need for detailed finding aids and participation in national consortia of linked databases disappears. The only descriptive tools that matter are those used by the archives staff to service the collection. With a large volume of records held by corporations, and small staffs to manage them, arrangement rarely goes below the folder level. Time management dictates that basic processing suffices in all but the most unusual circumstances.

The emergence of web-based technology has changed the face of information management in corporations. Fortified with skilled information systems personnel, intranet sites that limit access to company personnel and that house large collections of photographs, audio-visual files, and text records and have freed the archives staff from handling the Frequently Asked Questions to concentrate on mission-based initiatives. The emergence of the Internet as a tool for educating and entertaining has changed the mind-set of the researchers. Point and click technology enables people to get information that improves their personal lifestyle. The transition of this philosophy to the workplace shifts the burden of research to the individual, makes the archival holdings more relevant and accessible, and provides boundless opportunities for the archives to leverage this exposure to enhance its products and services.

Internet sites allow corporations new opportunities to interface with their consumers, customers, and shareowners, but the content must be compelling, engaging, and ever changing. From developing historical timelines highlighting the firm's milestones to providing brand histories and populating the website with interesting graphics, the archives should be a major contributor to this program. Unlike many other projects where the archives partners with other business units to meet a specific deadline, the need for new information is continual.

For the archivist, the web is an unparalleled opportunity for outreach to both internal and external audiences. For company personnel, the website functions as an interactive catalog of archival holdings, giving many associates their first exposure to this resource. For corporations with offices scattered across the globe, it allows the associates a point of direct interaction and provides new opportunities for collaboration. For outside researchers, an Internet site offers the best opportunity to slightly open the archival vault and share legacy with the general public. No company will post proprietary data, sensitive correspondence, or unedited marketing studies, but historical timelines, case studies, brand histories, advertising campaigns, summary financial documentation, company publications, news stories, policy statements, and executive speeches represent the broad spectrum of unique documentation available on corporate sites today. Over time, both the quality and quantity of these virtual archives will continue to expand, providing new research tools for business histories.

MARKETING THE ARCHIVES

Selling the merits of an archival program to business must be an ongoing, aggressive, and tactical activity. The inherent conflicts between the historical and the contemporary, heritage and innovation, often create a tension-filled atmosphere where the relevance and importance of history are often questioned if not attacked. To counter such attitudes, the archivist must continually promote the use of records as business tools for today's marketplace and provide convenient access to the collections. The corporate equivalent of a good finding aid may be a lobby exhibition, a feature story in an internal magazine, a well-designed page on an intranet/ Internet site, or training sessions that have an archival component. Building awareness and expanding the client-base may be the two most important objectives for every year's business plan.

Doing archival work in a corporation is akin to the discipline of a premier salesman. You identify clients one at a time, listen carefully to their specific needs, and customize programs that will satisfy them and contribute to their personal success. Word-of-mouth will then deliver other customers to the archival doorstep, and the cycle of mutual benefit can begin again. The first step in this process belongs to the archivist. Business units tend to be so focused on the present and on short-term gains that they do not consider historical perspectives as relevant factors in their planning.

The changing nature of the workforce itself also contributes to an ahistorical approach to marketing. Rapidly rotating managers who move easily between corporations have no sense of the products, services, marketing, or values that preceded their arrival. As the keeper of the corporate memory, the archivist has an opportunity to breach this knowledge gap and to act as a resource in the planning process.

The interchange can begin as an informal lunch, a get-acquainted informational exchange or as a personal tour of the archives, but the critical first step is to develop a relationship that can grow and mature as the client needs become clearer. In work settings where the operational mantra is to be "lean and mean," most effective managers will take full advantage of additional resources offered to them. By focusing on the particular needs of a department or group and developing delivery systems to make that information assessable, a mutually beneficial alliance has been created that results in better products for the company and wider support for the archives.

In identifying partnership opportunities, first look to relationships that have the most immediate and visible returns on a collaborative process. Public relations, corporate communications and the legal office are three areas that frequently require historical data to successfully fulfill their missions. They respect and appreciate the value of well-organized information that can be retrieved quickly. Access to such a resource has a direct impact on their ability to function quickly and accurately. Similarly, human resources, training, licensing, and consumer information groups recognize history as an asset that can improve and enhance their work products. More problematic are marketing, planning, technical, sales, and financial bodies who do not see obvious linkages for historical components in their work. From a practical standpoint, corporate archivists should gather apostles from the shared value-system groups first and use that base of support to recruit and enlist new converts.

In the business lexicon, the term "presence marketing" refers to the implementation of creative approaches to gain additional brand exposures in non-traditional advertising formats. Examples can include interactive signage at sports venues, branded experiences at theme parts and festivals, corporate sponsorships, and even banner advertising on the Internet. The underlying philosophy behind all these activities is to engage consumers where they work and play and make brands, products, and services a relevant part of their lives. Internalizing this approach will help to connect the archives more immediately and directly with its clients. A pervasive presence signals the importance of history and raises its visibility as a significant corporate asset. The enterprising archivist will aggressively seek out opportunities to market and promote heritage as a natural part of the business mosaic. From the physical location of the department to the programs it sponsors and the activities it supports, impressions about the archives are sent and received by the workforce. By focusing on a broad communications strategy, the archivist can positively influence these perceptions and improve organizational positioning. Such tools as publications, exhibitions, audio-visual productions, and historical presentations offer a broad spectrum of opportunities for outreach that both highlight the depth of the internal resource and encourage potential new users to the possibilities of partnering.

All corporations have anniversaries and milestones that mark key events in their history—events that can generate books, pamphlets, brochures, calendars, and other commemorative items that draw from the archival collection. These special events also create opportunities for producing oral histories and audio-visual productions to mark the events. By managing the history and establishing two-way communication with management on upcoming dates of note, the archives injects a historical component into the normal flow of business. Similarly, the use of exhibits will increase awareness of the archives and will signal its significance to associates. Lobby displays at headquarters, themed exhibits within departments, and showcases in the archives itself provide visual affirmation of the programs and encourage others to value past achievements and to consider contemporary projects from a historical perspective. Traveling exhibits can help link field offices to the corporate culture and can help build community interface with local cultural institutions and educational groups.

As a source of information for the media, the archives frequently functions as a powerful arm of the public relations department. From the photographic medium to radio and television advertising, documentary and training films, a well-organized archives with a strong service motivation can yield a harvest of positive publicity for the company and help to deliver key message points to targeted audiences. The archivist can become an adjunct member of the media relations staff by serving as company spokesperson on historical issues, thereby creating an expanded set of responsibilities that elevates the office and the importance of the function.

Outreach programs can also encompass orientation and training programs for associates; participation in speakers' bureaus that respond to external requests for presentations; the inclusion of historical features and photos in company magazines and newsletters; the creation of service awards using nostalgic imagery; the development of educational kits for instructional programs; and the creation of basic historical packages that can be adjusted for specific audiences and delivered by any associate. The key element in all of these endeavors is creativity and flexibility. Marketing is a continual process that adjusts to a changing work environment. It is pro-active and targeted towards specific measurable objectives. When close to 80 percent of corporate clients come to the archives by word of mouth, an emphasis on customer service will create those new opportunities that are the hallmarks of successfully managed programs.

THE BOTTOM LINE

Measuring value and quantifying returns on investment are evaluative processes that require strong discipline in their application. Using standard financial performance measuring sticks, the archives needs to account for the funds allocated to the function and provide a detailed stewardship report on results achieved. Whenever possible, these analyses should include a financial balance sheet showing the precise value of the services rendered. Business people fund programs on the basis of their value to the corporation. With intense competition for resources, only those projects with strong bottom lines will receive significant fiscal support.

Marketing professionals carefully calculate the anticipated returns that a consumer promotion or product launch will yield. Their business plans predict the anticipated market changes, and their managers are accountable for hitting the projected targets. Using a parallel scheme, archivists need to identify those institutional needs where documentation will support the business initiatives and where the archival contribution is apparent. In assigning work priorities and developing an operational mission, the intended results must have corresponding tools that allow for rigorous financial analysis.

Some programs will fit easily into a traditional profit and loss analysis, while others are softer and require a more creative assessment procedure. A licensing program that uses archival imagery to create nostalgic reproductions, housewares, toys, puzzles, or apparel would not exist without access to a well-managed historical image collection. The archives generates the resulting revenue stream and receives credit for it. In a typical licensing agreement, corporations receive royalty payments of 8 to 12 percent of wholesale sales. For licensing programs generating revenues in the millions of dollars, the archival contribution can easily exceed $1 million.

Other programs demand more innovative approaches in determining bottom-line contributions. For years, public relations firms have developed an accepted formula for evaluating results from publicity programs. Newspaper, magazine, radio, and television coverage of an event is assigned a value based on the costs of purchasing advertising in the same media. The costs of the program balanced against the media coverage value ensure a clear result. The program is either in the red or the black.

In a similar fashion, support for legal activities has measurable components. If outside legal research were required to provide documentation for pending litigation, the fees incurred would be based on a regional scale that is easily computed. In almost every instance, an in-house information specialist can locate and organize relevant documentation at a fraction of the costs required for similar services from the outside. The cost/value equation tilts strongly towards the internal resource.

Other support services for such programs as employee orientations, marketing promotions, consumer information, and community affairs can be more difficult to measure. In these circumstances, the archives is acting in the role of an outside vendor of services required to complete the project. With some research, it is possible to calculate project fees that would be charged by third party suppliers for the level of work. Such comparisons frequently will validate the cost benefits of an internal resource that can react more quickly and with greater accuracy than any outsourced company.

In a business environment where shareholders demand regular and increasing dividends on their investments and where chief executive officers have a very limited window in which to post positive results, the corporate archivist must create economic models that are powerful and persuasive to management. Every dollar allocated to an archival program should yield a return that will hold up under intense financial scrutiny. Initially, the development of a mindset that constantly analyzes projects on "return on investment" requires a very focused approach, but archivists who make it a part of their daily approach to projects dramatically improve their prospects for success.

Corporations spend millions of dollars on marketing research in an attempt to better understand their consumers and to deliver products that add value to their lives. Recognizing that their target audiences are constantly evolving, the research is ongoing and multi-dimensional, constantly monitoring the pulse of the client. For archivists working in a corporation, the parallels are compelling. To effectively sell products and services that are not core business functions requires strong marketing skills, a non-traditional approach to archival functions, and an understanding of how things work in the corporate world. Successful business archives programs embrace these guiding principles and seamlessly integrate their work product into a larger partnership that benefits clients and stakeholders alike.

7

Archival Programs in the Academic Library

Lauren R. Brown

INTRODUCTION

This chapter will draw heavily from my work experience and perceptions gained while working for over fifteen years as Curator of Archives and Manuscripts in the University of Maryland Libraries. The University of Maryland campus, located in College Park within the greater Washington, D.C. area, is positioned in a region densely packed with research repositories of national significance (Library of Congress, National Archives and Records Administration), a host of specialized repositories (AFL-CIO Archives, Folger Shakespeare Library), and numerous academic libraries (Johns Hopkins University, Georgetown University, and George Washington University, just to name a few). Our program has relationships with these institutions and with others in the region, such as the Maryland State Archives, which has delegated its responsibility for certain university-related archival records to our department on campus. Other departments within the University of Maryland Libraries, such as Marylandia and Rare Books, the National Trust for Historic Preservation Library Collection, and the Performing Arts Library, also have significant archival and special collections programs.

The last fifteen years have witnessed extraordinary growth within Archives and Manuscripts. The department has increased the size of its holdings dramatically from 8,000 linear shelf feet to a current total of approximately 30,000 linear feet of holdings. A 1985 researcher population of eighty visits per year to consult archival and manuscript holdings has expanded to a current population of over 1000 visits per year. At the same time distance assistance statistics have also skyrocketed with new forms of communication, such as e-mail, coming rapidly to the fore. The department staff has increased from three state budget line positions to a mix of state, contractual, and graduate assistantship positions that involve approximately fifteen employees. Programmatically, the department has continued to focus on its university archives program, on collecting personal papers and archival collections that document the history of Maryland, and in developing its labor history profile. At the same time it has launched new programs such as the National Public Broadcasting Archives, has brought in the Broadcast Pioneers Library of American Broadcasting, and has taken on administrative responsibility for literary manuscript collections (Katherine Anne Porter and Djuna Barnes among others) from another library department on campus.

I certainly would not pretend to claim more than a tiny portion of credit, if any, for the "success indicators" outlined above. Dedication, hard work, and vision displayed by colleagues in my department, effective support from key library and other campus administrators, strong interest and support given to the program by individual members of the faculty, and assistance obtained from a variety of non-campus individuals and organizations have all played significant roles. What follows, however, are some observations about characteristics in the work environment of an academic archives and manuscripts program that bear on the success or failure of such a program in present-day academe. Included as well are some thoughts on the dynamics of an archives program in a campus setting that hopefully will provide some new insights for those that are involved in academic archives.

ACADEMIC LIBRARIES—SOME CURRENT TRENDS

A significant number of academic library systems have implemented or are planning to implement faculty status for librarians, with a stated or implied opportunity for librarians and archivists to engage in scholarly research and writing. However, effective reference service and assistance to the library's clientele, broadly considered, continues to be the primary emphasis in academic libraries. This is not to suggest that archives can ignore their custodial role as guardians of valuable original source material or that archivists will not have an opportunity to engage in scholarly research and writing. But it has been my perception that the most important attribute, the one that will determine how an archival program is viewed both by the campus community and by professional colleagues in the library, will be the quality of reference service provided to users and the ability of users and other librarians to gain information about the holdings of the archive.

For this reason, stress should be placed on making the archives as accessible as possible, on attempting to provide a considerable amount of information about its holdings via the library's website or through other means, and on educating the campus community about research opportunities in the archival collections. Archivists should embrace and not oppose efforts by the library to make reference assistance to users in the library system as "seamless" as possible. Academic archivists should strive to "mainstream" information about archival holdings in bibliographic instruction within the library, to highlight those holdings in library publications, and to present information about archival collections in the library's online catalog. Rather than an afterthought after dealing with issues of collection development, arrangement and description, or preservation issues, archivists should assign a high priority to working on public service issues: the structuring of open hours, relationships with other public service points in the library system, the implications of providing distance assistance, the nature of the archives' clientele and how much assistance will be provided to them by archival staff, and how best to approach faculty and gain their interest in incorporating resources in the archival collections into their class curriculum. It is important to consider also that as part of an educational institution, academic archivists can and should play a key role in assisting novice users of original source materials and helping these users, many of them undergraduates, in acquiring research skills as they begin for the first time in their lives to make use of archival resources.

As part of a broader "environmental assessment," of an archival program, it is important to discuss the archives' service profile with supervisors and colleagues in the library, so there are no surprises or misunderstandings about the level of service being provided and the clientele that is being served. Inevitably, academic archives will attract a varied researcher population that extends far beyond the population of the campus. In the University of Maryland setting, visiting graduate students and faculty actually outnumber their campus equivalents in use of archival holdings (although campus undergraduates constitute the largest single segment of our user population). Certain holdings, such as literary manuscripts, attract a significant number of scholars from Europe and elsewhere in the world. There are certainly advantages in having a varied constituency that extends far beyond the immediate campus community if the leadership of the library sees its role as advancing scholarship generally and is inclined to be impressed at how campus archival and manuscript holdings have attracted the attention of a regional, national, or even a worldwide researcher constituency. Needless to say, however, it is crucial that the archival staff appreciates the value of providing top-notch assistance to students, faculty, and staff within campus community itself. The quality of service provided to campus administrators by the university archives program is particularly crucial. A balance will need to be achieved in this regard: there are ethical issues that should not be ignored involving equality of access to materials and resources in a research repository.

One important trend in the University of Maryland Libraries, and in many other academic libraries, is a strong move toward team-based work environments. Top-down decision making and hierarchical structures in the management sphere are to some extent giving way to staff "empowerment" as leadership is more broadly distributed through the rank and file of the staff. Typically, individual members of the library staff are becoming involved in working groups that address cross-functional or cross-departmental issues such as bibliographic instruction, collection development, and space planning.

Archival staff will be expected to participate in this process and to make a contribution to this team-based activity. In doing so, academic archivists will need to draw on skills that are perhaps only tangential to "pure" archival work such as arrangement and description or appraisal decisions. They will need to hone their facilitative leadership skills in meeting management, in space planning, in mediation and mentoring, in effective speaking and writing, and in time management, just to name a few. These skills will come into play outside the archival department but will also prove to be useful within the archives as well.

There may be occasions when the archivist may wonder if library-wide or even campus-wide committee and team-based assignments are unduly interfering with archives-specific issues and projects. However, one could view this management trend as a clear opportunity to shape the direction of key aspects of the entire library program and a way to demonstrate that archival staff can make important contributions to the library both outside as well as within the archival repository.

Certainly the impact of new technology has been and will continue to be an important arena in academic archives. The new web environment, scanning and digitization projects, and the increasing array of technical tools allowing for increased ease in providing distance assistance to researchers are all dramatically changing the way in which archivists carry out their work. For one new to the academic setting there may be surprise in discovering how involved academic units are in employing new technical tools to advance research and teaching. Another surprise might be the increasingly crowded array of digital projects involving libraries or library-related materials. Three could be cited among many: a three-year cooperative project among nine of the Big Ten universities to digitize nearly 3,000 works of American nineteenth-century fiction; a grant recently received by Cornell University to create an "online math archive" of selected publications in mathematics and statistics; and a project at MIT Libraries to build a digital archive capable of holding the approximately 10,000 articles produced by MIT authors annually. Archival programs are increasingly likely to be able to find resources on campus needed to initiate digital projects; if anything archivists may be put under increased pressure to contribute ideas and/or content towards library or library consortium initiatives. Archivists may quickly realize that there are advantages in forming partnerships with rare books curators or other special collections departments on campus (or in the region) in pursuing digital projects.

Acquiring and archiving electronic records of permanent value, not only those generated by the campus, but also those generated by individuals and outside organizations, will continue to pose a serious challenge to archival programs.

What has been described above has significant implications for new staff hires. While finding candidates who have benefitted from formal instruction in archives and have excelled in archival work will continue to be important, so to will be attributes such as the ability to show creativity and flexibility, the ability to work productively in team environments, the ability to work effectively in an increasingly diverse work environment, and certainly a high level of familiarity with personal computers and relevant software applications. Archivists will want to look for new employees who have potential for operating more or less independently on certain assignments, who do not shy away from accepting responsibilities, and who are also committed to participating in a work environment that depends heavily on open lines of communication, close cooperation with others, and the ability to compromise.

THE CAMPUS, THE LIBRARY LEADERSHIP, AND THE ARCHIVES

It may be surprisingly obvious to those who reflect on this that the library director or dean is in a peer group that does not include any librarians or archivists. By this I mean that the other academic deans, the provost, and other senior administrative officers on campus are not engaged in library or archival work and may be too busy or lack the inclination to become fully conversant with how libraries and archives really function. In addition, senior campus administrators may demonstrate only lukewarm interest at best in their support of the library's program, which can be perceived as competing with other urgent campus priorities. In fact, academic libraries, involving significant physical plant needs, labor-intensive staff activity, and exploding publication costs, might be viewed as financial black holes that perhaps deserve lip service ("the heart of the university") but present demands to the campus that of necessity need to be strictly contained. This fact should not be lost on the rank and file of the library staff, including the staff of the archives. Too often there is a temptation on the part of academic archivists to criticize or blame the library administration for what is perceived as inadequate staffing or material support of archival endeavors when it is more imperative to close ranks with the leadership of the library and present a united front for supporting the entire library program when interacting with campus administration and with key campus constituencies.

Whatever can be done to increase the effectiveness and success of the top library administration by library archivists should be done—whether it is timely delivery of information located in the university archives, news about campus developments passed on to the library leadership, or lobbying on behalf of general library initiatives as well as those which more directly effect the archival program. It is also important to become attuned to formally-stated goals and objectives of the campus and to discern the relationship of library and archival programs to the campus mission statement or broadly-recognized campus objectives. Archivists should perceive themselves as part of this process—in building a positive view of the library program, educating key members of the campus community about issues and opportunities connected with that program, and being in a position to talk intelligently about all major aspects of the library's operations—and not assuming that this is a task that the library director or dean should undertake completely on their behalf.

Archivists who are involved with soliciting personal or organizational papers should be prepared to talk knowledgeably to outsiders about any campus program, initiative, or event being covered in the local or national news media. For example, I joined one of my colleagues in visiting the home of a local environmentalist who held organizational records dealing with environmental issues in Maryland. Before donating these files to the University of Maryland, she was very interested in my insights about a wetlands controversy that then existed involving an edge of our campus. Fortunately, I was prepared to hold an intelligent discussion on that topic, which involved the U.S. Army Corps of Engineers, state government and campus officials, and student organizations.

Forging a productive relationship with the teaching faculty is crucial but may present unique challenges. Certain faculty may have such a high interest in libraries and such a high expectation of the campus library in terms of presentation of scholarly information and services that they may be very difficult to satisfy. However, archivists should understand the symbiotic relationship that can and should exist between librarians and academics and seize opportunities to engage in collaborative efforts involving teaching, collection development, and research. For example, faculty can provide insights and information about current scholarly research trends, which may have implications for the collection development profile in the archives program. Alliances can be forged with individual professors or academic departments that may either effectively promote or protect desired archival initiatives. Certainly the relationship between the archives program and a campus library school or history department that offers formal instruction in archives or manuscripts curatorship is of crucial importance. Here one obviously finds high potential for a mutually productive relationship involving classroom instruction, student internships, and the hiring of student assistants who are looking at archives work as a career choice.

A few basic precepts are in order as one develops a working relationship with senior library leadership or campus administrators. Try to avoid "the negatives" in presenting a case for support to resource allocators. I have found it a rare occasion when an administrator makes a positive, supportive decision after hearing about "disastrous consequences" if that decision is not made, or in being "shamed" into making what archival staff might perceive to be the "right" decision. Far more productive, I believe, is expressing clearly the positive benefits, not just for the archival program but for the library generally, that will flow out of a decision to provide additional support—be it more staffing, funding for the acquisition or processing of collections, or additional equipment. Any problem brought to the attention of an administrator should be coupled with at least one proposed solution to that problem. Try to anticipate crises coming to the fore, either in the immediate archival program or some element of the library program, and be prepared in advance to suggest constructive ways in which the library (or by extension, the campus) can deal with that crisis. Don't insist on a certain communication channel; experiment with a variety of techniques (e-mail, phone communication, face-to-face meetings) to see which venue seems to hold the most promise. I have known certain administrators who will completely ignore a certain means of communication but will respond positively to another. Be as scrupulously honest in your dealings with others as possible. An incident exposing lack of honesty or credibility may quickly undermine years of accumulated trust.

As one seeks to expand the number of staff members, successful results may ensue if one can secure sources of outside funds and then ask the library or the campus administration to consider funding a portion of the costs needed to "realize" a given staff position or project. Once having secured additional staff, it is at times possible to advertise the benefits for the library in retaining a contractual employee. This option hinges on how much effort has been made to hire an outstanding individual and in presenting that employee as a talented member of the library team who is making a substantial contribution to the library organization and consequently should be retained. It is important not to be perceived as hoarding staff resources in the archives and "building an empire" in the process. On occasion we have had talented contractual or student assistant staff who have decided to migrate to other positions in the library organization; this has generally produced a very positive impression in the library and has certainly assisted in forging alliances with other units in the library system, such as the Friends of the Libraries office or our technical services division.

It is important to build a "sense of excitement" about archival programs and initiatives. In this instance, one's immediate setting may dictate different decisions on how excitement can be generated in the minds of colleagues in the library and on campus generally. Usually library publication editors are more than pleased to receive articles on new acquisitions, special events, and exhibits involving an archival program. In our case we have been generally successful in capturing thirty percent of the copy space used for a publication sent to members of the library friends organization. We also have enjoyed a strong presence in a publication that is routed to library staff. When asked, campus-wide publication editors have been generally receptive to printing articles or photo spreads about our archival program.

Certainly, well-organized and well-attended public events that serve to forge closer ties between the archival program and outside constituencies can enhance the archival program, particularly if these events also involve the library dean and other campus officers who are asked to participate. A key consideration here is to think out well in advance who stands to benefit from these events and who deserves public recognition as the event proceeds. Exhibits should be designed in a way so that viewers come away with the perception that they have really experienced or learned something and have not just observed historical artifacts on display.

CONCLUSION

A library environment where team management prevails and a strong service orientation exists does not preclude the need to make strategic use of available staff resources for archives-specific projects. Being able to set priorities while retaining a measure of flexibility to meet changing circumstances and opportunities will continue to play a crucial role.

Crucial also will be the need to be attuned to evolving means of dissemination of information in libraries while still remaining true to core values of archivists and curators—preserving and making available documentary information of long-term value, preserving the institutional memory of the campus (if the archival program is responsible for the university archives program), ensuring the proper care of unique historical artifacts, and supporting scholarly research. In fact, archivists in an academic setting will discover that they will have many opportunities to promote archival methodologies as time progresses. Particularly with digital projects, archivists will have a clear opportunity to influence decisions on both the content of material presented digitally and the way in which that presentation is structured.

It is sometimes difficult to predict what the information and management landscape will be like on academic campuses in the future. From my perspective, however, team-management concepts are here to stay and for this reason there will be ongoing importance placed in fostering close collaborative relationships with other library staff and other individuals on campus. A college or a university is truly a "learning organization," and as part of this, archivists will need to be attentive to the importance of continually gaining new job skills (and not necessarily skills peculiar to archives work) in order to stay abreast of the times.

Administering an archival program in an academic library will continue to require a blend of archival, negotiating, and leadership skills. As one negotiates a path through a campus environment that might be described as a very complex social organization, one should not lose sight of the fact that libraries, and by extension archives in library settings, are primarily information providers and will be ultimately judged on how well they succeed in making scholarly information readily accessible and in how successful they are in providing high-quality service to campus constituencies. Customer responsiveness, quality service, and attentiveness to the library, the university, and the research community as a whole will be the hallmarks of successful programs.

8

Leadership of Archival Programs

Bruce W. Dearstyne

LEADERSHIP AND THE STATE OF ARCHIVAL PROGRAMS

The archival mission is immensely important because of its implications for documenting the development and operation of important institutions, for ensuring the availability of records of enduring value for research, and for fostering the transmission of culture and values from one generation to the next. "History is not what happened in the past. It is, as the word itself suggests, a story written by subsequent generations," the Society of American Archivists reminds us. "The veracity and accuracy of the account, however, is totally dependent on the surviving record at hand—documents, manuscripts, letters, publications, photos, and memorabilia—from which the story must often be pieced together and reconstructed, item by item, clue by clue."[1] Archives also play a vital role as sources for administrative continuity, as legal documents, and in other ways essential to institutions.

The importance of the archival mission means that the *leadership* of archival programs is an important issue. It is leadership that provides direction, fosters progress, and helps ensure success. But the evidence suggests that there is room for improvement in the area of archival leadership. A majority of archival programs in the United States are underdeveloped or at best modestly resourced in comparison to the importance and magnitude of the work they are charged to carry out.[2] The work is demanding; leading even a small archival program requires dealing with records creators and do-nors, facilities and equipment, people (your boss, your staff), researchers, information technology, and other issues, often more or less simulta-neously! At the same time, the archival profession and the field broadly de-fined are also undergoing change. The traditional ways of doing things are not always effective, and program direction requires more independent and improvisation than ever before. Leadership requires confronting and mastering a series of archival dilemmas (see Table 8.1).

This chapter focuses on *leadership* and begins with an assumption that it is similar to, but different from, *management*. In most archival programs, the person at the top needs to exhibit a blend of the two but also to realize the differences between them. Leaders are change agents; they envision a better future for their programs, articulate goals, inspire employees, repre-

Table 8.1

Archival mission	At the same time
Serve the parent institution	Serve the causes of history and heritage
Collaborate with librarians, records managers, other information professionals	Maintain a distinct professional archival identity and profile
Continue the archival tradition and archival theory and precepts	Change and adapt with the times and develop new approaches for new problems
Operate with the realization that the function has great importance	The function may not be well understood and supported
Identify from the past and the present what will be valued and used in the future	No one can fully anticipate what will interest or engage people in the future
Identify and preserve those records of continuing value	You can't know the entire universe of documentation
Preserve and prolong the useful life of records and information	The media are fragile and will not last forever
Capitalize on the benefits of the infor-mation revolution and electronic records	Electronic information may be transitory; electronic records are often deleted by their creators
Maintain the concept of a *record* as something that is fixed, recorded, identifiable	Realize that the concept is undermined and possibly irrelevant in electronic systems

sent needs clearly, advocate passionately, and have a flair for program building. They gaze out at the horizon, yearn for the future, and think in terms of change. They have a sense of *destiny*. Managers, by contrast, are well organized, focus on the work at hand, are performance-and-outcome oriented by nature, and pride themselves in getting the work done. They are more likely to gaze at the annual workplan (or the clock) than at the horizon, yearn for finishing a particular project on time and within budget, and think in terms of concrete deliverables and products. They have a sense of *let's get it done*. In Warren Bennis' memorable phrase, the leader *does the right thing* while the manager *does things right*.[3]

Despite the importance of leadership and management, the archival profession has given only limited attention to either one. Of course, some archival program directors reach leadership positions from outside the field; their leadership abilities may be well developed by the time they take over as head of the program. But the majority come from within the field. Many professional archivists reach management positions relatively early in their careers, no surprise given the fact that many of the programs are small or modest in scope. In many instances, they lack leadership or management training and, once they reach management levels, may lack the time or the inclination to acquire any. There are a number of reasons for this rather curious phenomenon. Models of excellence in archival leadership are scarce. Professional associations offer relatively little in the way of leadership or management training beyond occasional one-day workshops. Articles on management in journals such as the *American Archivist* are rare; there is only one publication exclusively devoted to management, in the SAA's "Archival Fundamentals" series. Articles on archival leadership are even more rare.

Some archivists assume that management really does not require any special training, that it is little more than the application of common sense principles. Some professional archivists feel that there is an incompatibility between being a *professional* and being a *manager*. Professionals, they feel, need to be concerned with the application of professional theories and principles; managers with getting the job done in the least possible time at the lowest possible cost. One may play the role of a manager, but the main challenge, according to this type of reasoning, is to hold onto one's professional archival roots and high standards. Finally, some people in this field simply doubt their ability to be effective leaders; they feel they lack the personal assertiveness, energy, or ability to engage and inspire and conclude that these things cannot be developed and learned. In other cases, people try to play a leadership role, for instance, through initiating dramatic new ventures, only to fail or fall short and, chastened by the experience, to become much more circumspect and cautious. As a consequence of all of this, many archival programs are not very well managed and, as a whole, these programs tend to be *under-led*.

Leadership *matters* in archival programs in the same sense that it does in other institutions, including government and politics (see Appendices A and B at the end of this chapter). It is the leader who more than any other person gives direction and meaning to the program. It is the skill and ability of the leader, more than any other set of factors, that determines how well the program works and what it delivers. Leaders give life to their programs. Leadership is needed to address at least three questions on a more or less continual basis:[4]

- *Why are we here?* The organization's mission is always open to question from employees and stakeholders. Questions keep it vivid and alive, help it keep pace with changing realities, and make it worthy of attention and support.

- *What's going on here?* Why are we doing things the way we do? Organizations must be committed to constant change, and not merely as an abstract principle. They must question their environment and status daily in order to keep up.

- *Where are we headed?* Are we making progress? In order to be accountable to stakeholders for accomplishing their mission, organizations must *manage for results*. Careful planning and measurement, constant monitoring of quality and continual debate over the nature of indicators keep organizations focused on goals and tasks.

A good deal of leadership work is "outward-focused"—it relates to getting attention, building alliances, garnering resources, and generally helping the program prosper in its institutional context. From a different perspective, leaders are supposed to *serve* their programs. "The first responsibility of a leader is to define reality," says Max DePree. "The last is to say thank you. In between the two, the leader must become a servant and a debtor. That sums up the progress of an artful leader." Leaders need to work to leave behind assets and a legacy. They need to impart such things as a sense of quality in the program's work, to ensure that it is open to influence, to make sure it changes with the times. They need to develop a "corporation rationality" that provides the basis for "reason and mutual understanding" of what the program is trying to accomplish. Leaders *owe* their employees space to work and grow and opportunities for professional development. Leaders are obligated to provide momentum—"the feeling among a group of people that their lives and work are intertwined and moving toward a recognizable and legitimate goal." Leaders are responsible for effectiveness and output, but they also must develop, express, and defend "civility and values" and "to make a meaningful difference in the lives of those who permit leaders to lead."[5]

MARKS OF EXCELLENCE

Strong, well-led programs feature adequate support, sufficient (and rising) funding, clear direction, appropriate staffing, and secure facilities. Such programs are usually characterized by several features, summarized below.[6]

Clear Sense of Purpose and Mission

The strongest, best-led programs have a clear sense of what business they are in and what they intend to accomplish. Usually, this is developed through the envisioning work of the leader and through a participatory planning process that he or she leads. It is embodied in guiding documents, including operating charters, mission, and vision statements, and strategic plans that set forth goals, objectives, and priorities. These foundation documents are fundamentally important as indicators of well-thought-out, settled purposes. But more important, the sense of purpose and mission are clear in the hearts and minds of employees, clear to the people to whom the director of the program reports, and clear to other key constituents such as trustees. The program has a sense of steadiness and mastery.

Evolution and Change

The strongest programs tend to be more or less continually "on the move"—their makeup and priorities this year are different from what they were last year and next year they will evolve still further. They regard change as a norm, accept and welcome it, and use it to their advantage. The leaders of these programs perceive that our society, economy, and institutions are all in the midst of significant change that never seems to stop. The parent institutions of the archival programs are caught up in change; the nature of the records themselves is changing, particularly with the shift to digital technology; the makeup of the research community and traffic is undergoing changes, particularly with the shift to Web-based access and services; and the nature of the research use is also evolving. The most successful programs hold onto what works but at the same time keep changing to accommodate new challenges and needs.

Dynamic, Balanced Expansion

The best archival programs not only change; they also tend to *grow* over time. Growth is a natural trait for a dynamic archival program: its accessions steadily increase and the number of users steadily grows. But there is an additional element of aspiration and stretch in the best-led, most dynamic programs. They seek out new missions (related to what they are already doing), provide new services, fill service vacuums (for instance, providing records management services that complement their ongoing archival work), and seek to form partnerships. They proceed slowly, responsibly, and strategically, building alliances and support and garnering additional recognition, respect, and resources as they grow. They reason that it is worth at least a small risk to expand in the sense that dynamic expansion coupled with good works are likely to attract more resources. All of the programs described in the other chapters in this book are good examples of the inclination toward expansion.

High Visibility

The best programs are not shy or cloistered. They are well known within their parent institutions, familiar to users, and noticed within the archival field. They actively call attention to their holdings and services and to the importance of the archival function generally, through newsletters, publications, exhibits, conferences, news releases, videos, websites, and other devices. They repeatedly issue reports even when there is no explicit requirement for them to do so just because they want to engage certain audiences. They cultivate a relationship with the local news media. Their goal is to catch the attention of current and potential customers, resource allocators, and decision makers whose actions affect the fate of the archival program, and others with a potential interest in archives. They reason that applying resources to outreach and marketing efforts is a sound investment decision even if it means (as it inevitably does) applying commensurately fewer resources to mainline archival work such as appraisal and processing. Strong programs recognize that there is a tradeoff, and they opt for promotional marketing efforts on the reasoning that they will have long-term payoffs for the program.

Customer Focus

The best led programs in this business have a clear focus on their customers—the individuals, groups, and institutions they aim to serve. Customers include people who produce archival records, researchers who use them, and to a degree the parent institution of which the archival program is a part. "Pleasing the customer" is a fundamental operating assumption of the best led programs. They put away the notion that archives are a monopoly and that people therefore need to use them no matter the quality of the service. They consistently provide quick, accurate, responsive service. In this sense, their leaders regard archives as a *business* that must have excellent service as its hallmark in order to survive and prosper. The best programs probe customer views, interests, and needs in many ways: direct discussion (for instance, in the search room), questionnaires that measure satisfaction and seek suggestions, focus groups, inviting e-mail comments via their websites, and keeping up with the literature on customer preferences and trends. They regard customers as partners—important but not exclusive providers of information and advice on how the programs should evolve and change. Part of "customer focus" is integrating advice from customers with information from professional associations, the parent agency, and other sources to arrive at decisions on how to proceed—in effect, sensing and identifying what customers need before they realize it themselves. That is part of the leadership role in the area of customer service.

Peer Recognition

Perhaps the best way to identify strong archival programs is simply to ask around at a professional archival conference. The archival community generally recognizes the best programs through such things as reading and quoting their written reports and products, interacting with their staffs at professional conferences, cooperating in projects with them, observing how they deal with difficult issues such as handling archival electronic records, hearing good things about them from researchers, and emulating or simply copying what they do. More formal mechanisms, particularly the Society of American Archivists' Distinguished Service Award, identify the very best programs in the field.

Professional Engagement

Strong programs and active professional involvement have for many years been associated with each other and tend to be mutually reinforcing. People from excellent programs contribute their time and talents to professional associations as a form of sharing with their colleagues, a chance to learn from others, and a means of advancing the field in general. People from the best programs are often called on to give papers at professional conferences and write for professional journals and regard it as a natural part of their work to contribute in this way; conversely, they understand that professional engagement is a way to learn. Professional associations also provide a mechanism for cooperative ventures and a forum for dealing with some of the most difficult archival problems such as managing electronic archival records. The strongest programs tend to be marked by their commitment to the profession and their realization that the well-being of the profession and the well-being of programs associated with it are mutually reinforcing.

LEADERSHIP OF SUCCESSFUL ARCHIVAL PROGRAMS

Leaders of successful archival programs—leaders exemplified by the authors of the other chapters in this book—exhibit a knack for program development and advancement. Leadership is something that can be developed and learned, but it requires study, concentration, and work. Several of the most important aspects of archival leadership are discussed below. This discussion has much in common with the themes that come through in the other chapters.

Politically Savvy

All archival programs operate in institutional settings and most are parts of some office or agency within those institutions such as an information center, records management office, library, or museum. Much of the leader's time is of necessity spent in communicating, advocating, negotiating, and sometimes pleading with people outside the archives who have a measure of influence over its destiny. The best archival leaders are good politicians in the sense that they are aware of their institutional surroundings, understand how things get done in their parent organizations, know how to exert influence, recognize when to compromise, and have the communications and interpersonal skills to do all of those things and stay on good terms with their own bosses. The following list summarizes effective political approaches of the best archival program leaders:

1. Works at staying on good terms with his or her own supervisor though such approaches as being forthright, seeking guidance on personal improvement, building trust and confidence by ensuring that the archival program gets results, and whenever possible making sure the archival program reinforces broader institutional goals. The archival program director and his or her supervisor won't always agree, and there will be times when the director doesn't tell the supervisor everything that is going on! But the relationship has to be one of mutual respect and openness if the archival program is to develop and thrive.

2. Works hard at understanding the operational context in which the parent agency is operating, e.g., its program priorities, the problems it is facing, how it is regarded by key decision makers and resource allocators (e.g., the university trustees, state legislature, or corporate board of directors), how its business is changing, critical issues in the field, and best practices and programs in the field.

3. Develops and works through a network of advisory groups which provide insight about program operation, advise on new services, and also serve as advocacy engines for the program. As noted below, part of archival leadership is operating within a series of networks that help give the program buoyancy and direction.

4. Develops and maintains contacts among key decision makers and resource allocators. As Larry Hackman in particular points out, archival leadership often succeeds because of the cultivation of contacts with a few well-placed, interested, influential individuals: the trustee who is interested in the university's history, the state legislator who feels strongly that good government and archives are related, the assistant to the president who is interested in electronic records management.

5. Develops, refines, and constantly practices excellent communication skills, particularly oral skills, concentrating on explaining the values, needs, and plans of his or her program in terms that are concise, understandable, and compelling. Perhaps the most important and highly regarded skill of a leader is the ability to speak eloquently, concisely, and in terms that are descriptive, moving, and uplifting.

6. Understands the value of persistence. Part of archival leadership is simply the ability to stay focused and determined despite disappointments and setbacks over time and to keep everyone focused on the fact that the archives takes a long-range view of things. Some of the most successful programs owe much of their success to the patience of leaders who kept up a steady and ultimately persuasive message about program development needs, who kept revising and pushing the budget initiative request until it finally succeeded, who cultivated relationships, who worked for several years to get a partnership developed and operating.

7. Understands the value of confidential negotiations and also the value of open bargaining, and knows when to use each one to advantage. Archival leaders know when quiet diplomacy is likely to be most effective, when to go public, and how to blend and balance the two.

8. Senses that leadership may go through a cycle: initial energy and new direction, sustained achievement, and then either continual progress or else a gradual lapse and loss of momentum. It is difficult to be a dynamic leader for a long period of time: the mission gets achieved and the excitement wanes; leaders lose their energy and edge; staying too long brings too much familiarity and a fatigue factor sets in (people simply get tired of the leader). Sometimes, the best service the leader can do for the program is to move on to something else and make way for someone new.

Defining the Vision for the Program

"There is no more powerful engine driving an organization toward excellence and long-range success than an attractive, worthwhile, and achievable future, widely shared. . . . Effective leaders have agendas. . . . They adopt challenging new visions of what is both possible and desirable, communicate these visions, and persuade others to become so committed to these new directions that they are eager to lend their resources and energies to make them happen."[7] This aspect of leadership requires a sense of the parent institution's goals and priorities, an understanding of how to connect the destiny of the archival program to those goals and priorities, a feeling for where the field is headed, a familiarity with best practices and programs in the field that can serve as approximate models, and an ability to describe the destination: what the program will look like if it achieves its potential. Vision always relates to the future; it is a way of transcending everyday issues and problems and focusing on potential for transformation and growth. The right vision attracts attention, encourages commitment, energizes people, and makes the program notable to outsiders who recognize and respect its freshness and spirit.

Keeping Archives in the *Change* Business

Few archival programs have a totally satisfactory status quo. If they are satisfied they may in fact have entered a state of complacency, which is dangerous. For the most part *change* is what is needed. But change is unsettling and uncomfortable; it threatens to change the nature of the work, relationships, and traditional ways of doing things, and to bring or force new learning and new approaches. Leaders of change-adept organizations have the imagination to innovate, an inclination to make connections, and an understanding of the resources that will be needed to perform. This requires passion, conviction, and confidence in others. The first step is tuning into the environment, gathering and analyzing information, and discerning where change is needed. Next, they challenge the prevailing organizational wisdom by considering all the information at hand and manipulating it to form new patterns—new ways of looking at the program, how it delivers services, who its customers are, options for serving them. They need to communicate a compelling sense of the vision—one that appeals to everyone to collectively become something more than they are. The next step is building coalitions with people who have the resources, the knowledge, and the political savvy and clout to make things happen. Then comes the difficult task of getting managers and others to take ownership and move ahead; this includes giving people lots of leeway in how they approach implementation of the vision.[8] The changed approaches need to be monitored, nurtured, and to take root deeply in the corporate culture of the program. Probably the most common explanation for why transformation efforts fail is that leaders declare victory too soon, relax, move on to other things, or settle into the relatively comfortable role of managing the new status quo.

But in fact, the new ways are not sufficiently anchored in the corporate culture. The old, inadequate ways reappear, people go back to doing things the way they did in the past, the entire program sags, and much of the leader's work is gradually undone.[9]

Archival leaders dealing with the complex challenge of effecting change can gain insight from business practices. They need to build *adaptive organizations* that constantly monitor the environment and sense changing realities, recognize that change is evolutionary and that the program helps create the future even as it moves into it, acknowledge the presence of uncertainty, and understand the advantages of being opportunistic within the broad parameters of the program's vision, mission, and goals. They understand that their program operates in multiple, evolving contexts and that the leader therefore needs to be adept at taking a sense-and-respond approach. Programs achieve this approach to things through encouraging individual learning, sharing and leveraging the learning within the program, keeping focused on the outside landscape rather than the internal politics of the organization, valuing a diversity of people and opinions, and encouraging responsible risk-taking.[10]

Valuing Employees

Leaders work actively and tirelessly with and for the employees of their programs, particularly professional employees. The reason should be obvious: archival programs are small to modest in size and there isn't an employee to spare! Everyone's time, talent, energy, and insights are needed. Archivists as a group tend to be highly motivated, talented, proud of their work, and dedicated to the cause of archives. On the other hand, they are affected by shifts in perspectives and relationships that are impacting the workforce as a whole, including reorganizations, farming out operations where internal expertise is lacking, and the tendency toward lean organizations. Chain of command is less important than expertise and ability in gaining respect and recognition; there may be less interest than in the past in climbing the institutional ladder and more in acquiring transportable skills and reputations; and there may be stronger attachments to the profession and particular projects than to the program as a whole.[11] Given this complicated pattern, leaders spend a good deal of their time recruiting, developing, and fostering the work of employees. The series of questions below measures some of the core elements needed to attract, focus, and keep talented employees:[12]

1. Do I know what is expected of me at work?
2. Do I have the materials and equipment I need to do my work right?

3. At work do I have the opportunity to do what I do best every day?

4. In the last seven days, have I received recognition or praise for doing good work?

5. Does my supervisor, or someone at work, seem to care about me as a person?

6. Is there someone at work who encourages my development?

7. At work, do my opinions count?

8. Does the mission/purpose of my company make me feel my job is important?

9. Are my coworkers committed to doing quality work?

10. Do I have a best friend at work?

11. In the last six months, has someone at work talked to me about my progress?

12. In the last year, have I had opportunities to learn and grow?

Extensive training and development opportunities, including taking courses and attending professional conferences, are helpful in keeping employees engaged and energetic. Decentralized decision-making and a policy of empowerment that puts responsibilities with staff members for implementation of policies and figuring out how to solve problems and get the work done are good approaches to development and to encouraging everyone to take initiative and identify with the work.

The best archival leaders also recognize that they can't always use such incentives as salary increases and promotions to help motivate people. Another powerful strategy is deployed: genuine interest in employees and praise for their work. "Appreciation, acknowledgment, praise, thank you's, some simple gesture that says 'I care about you and what you do.' . . . information that communicates 'You're on the right track. You're doing really well. Thanks.' . . . The heart of effective leadership is genuinely caring about people."[13] Besides personal attention, recognition and praise, leaders create, encourage, and participate in forums and opportunities for celebration and raising the level of comradery: going out to lunch, celebrating major accomplishments (e.g., the installation of a new automated system, the launching of the archival website, a major new exhibit, a sizeable budget increase); special recognitions or citations for individual or team accomplishments; encouraging socializing off the job (the employee softball or bowling team); program logos and t-shirts; and celebrating personal milestones such as birthdays. Are such approaches really suited to such a high-minded, serious calling as archives? The answer is *yes*, provided they are genuine, sincere, and consistent.

Developing Employees

One of the most important strategies is to foster the development of new sets of knowledge, skills, and abilities in professional employees. These extend well beyond such things as archival competency, understanding how to manage electronic records, and generally how to do the work. They focus on more subtle, less definable traits that are essential for professionals in this field. These include:

Analysis/conceptualization. Professionals in archival programs need to develop skills to enable them to understand the business of the archival program's parent agency, perceive patterns and relationships, break problems down, understand how traditional archival approaches fit the challenges at hand, and realize when an innovative solution is needed. Sometimes, the challenge is to reconceptualize the problem, look at it in a new way, and thereby gain insight into how it might be solved.

Communication. Leaders need to be excellent communicators; professionals in programs also need skills in this area. Much of the success in archives depends on two types of communication skills: (1) ability to articulate and dramatize the archival mission and function in compelling terms that engage people who are not archival professionals; (2) draw out and understand others, including bosses and customers, who may find it difficult to articulate their wants and needs. As noted above, communication skills of a high order are essential in leaders, but they are also important in all employees.

Teaching/clarifying. A good deal of archival work seems mysterious or complicated to non-archivists. Issues associated with digital information technology and electronic records are particularly challenging. Part of the challenge is to *teach* in the basic sense of conveying information, bringing enlightenment, answering questions, mediating among people, finding aids and records, and generally lifting the level of understanding. Archival professionals need to cut through complexity, explain such mysterious matters as electronic archival records and help people understand archival and related information management issues.

Understanding use and users. Increasingly, archival professionals need to be experts on *use*: how people derive and conceptualize their information needs, how they seek out information, what it takes to satisfy an information need, how to balance printed/published sources vs. primary sources such as archives and how the Internet and the Web change all of this. *User centeredness* needs to become a watchword.

Understanding potential and impact of technology. Archivists do not need to become computer experts but they do need to understand major information technology trends and developments; the impact of such major trends as the shift to digital records and access over the Web; and how archives need to tailor their programs to respond. They also need to understand the technological tools of the trade, e.g., software used to describe and provide access to archival records.

Partnering for Progress

Archival programs can make headway through partnering with other programs and reaching out for allies. Some of the best programs operate as part of networks which effectively augment their modest resources and extend their reach and influence. The role needs to transcend serving, advising, and regulating to partnering, cooperating, and coordinating. As Larry Hackman's chapter points out, one of the most effective approaches is to create a series of advisory committees and boards which articulate customer viewpoints, broaden the program's perspectives, advise it on how to proceed, and, perhaps most important of all, also function as advocacy groups for the program. An advisory committee that also effectively lobbies for the program can make a major difference at critical junctures: new legislation or regulations to redefine the program, major expansion into new areas, significant budget initiatives. Partnering with key offices, e.g., records management, CIO (Chief Information Officer), library, counsel (which may want archival records for litigation purposes), public relations (as Phil Mooney points out, archival records are helpful for advertising and other public relations purposes), and others.

Archivists also need to partner with allied information professionals if they are to make progress with digital records:

Today's conceptualization of who and what the information professions comprise has expanded and diversified in direct relation to the expanded conceptualization of what kinds of information resources and services make up or should make up the digital environment. This broadened conceptualization encompasses everyone who manages information content as well as those who design, document, and exploit information context and structure. This includes librarians, archivists, curators, preservationists, technical information specialists, and information systems and museum professionals. The important roles played by the creators of digital information are also being recognized. The drive to develop transparent, networked, multimedia, multi-repository resources has brought these professional communities and information creators into a new metacommunity. The members of this metacommunity are converging around issues of metadata standards and interoperability, electronic record-keeping systems design, interface design, intellectual property, and professional education.[14]

Inspiring by Example

Personal drive and energy are important factors. Leaders of the best archival programs seem to be energized and given vitality by the work itself. They relish the work, exhibit a genuine passion for it, consistently apply energy and good judgment, and willingly put in lots of extra time. They seem to never tire! They put the program's good ahead of their own good; they are ambitious for the program's progress rather than for personal advancement or gain. They give and share credit and praise; they tend to take the blame when things go wrong. "The leaders who work most effectively . . . never say 'I'. . . . They think 'we'; they think 'team.' They understand that their job is to make the team function. . . . There is an identification (very often, quite unconscious) with the task and with the group. This is what creates trust, what enables you to get the work done." But this approach needs to be balanced by the realization that the leader's job is to make a difference. "What do I want to be remembered for?" is the key, motivating question.[15]

Lifting the Archival Field

Leaders of the strongest, most prominent programs are not only active at home; they also acknowledge that no archival program is an island and that they have an obligation to help change and strengthen the archival field. Major change will continue to be the order of the day: the quantity and importance of electronic records will continue to increase dramatically, many services and interactions with customers will move to the Web, more effective approaches to documentation and selection of archival records from the overabundant mass of contemporary information will need to be developed, the need to clarify and assert the nature of archives in a complex information environment will intensify, and the competition for attention and resources is unlikely to abate. Leaders of archival programs need to find time to apply their insights and talents in at least two directions. One, they need to support and play leadership roles in professional associations. These associations are challenged as never before in attracting younger members (who may value professional recognition less than their parents' generation), in meeting member needs (which members themselves may find it difficult to articulate and which are constantly changing), in producing publications and guidelines in a timely fashion (difficult to do in the area of digital technology where the issues and needs morph and change faster than associations can get out guidelines to address them), and in deciding how best to render services (are publications and professional conferences gradually being upstaged by the Internet and the Web?)

The second area where statesmanlike leadership is needed is cooperation with other programs. Even the best archival programs have shown an inclination to go it alone rather than cooperate in such obvious areas as collecting policies and despite the fact that resource constraints might lead logically to strategies for dividing the work and pooling resources. Probably the best mechanism for cooperation are the state historical records advisory boards that operate in each state under the coordination of the state archivists and with the sanction and support of the National Historical Publications and Records Commission. Statewide strategic plans developed under these boards during the past decade provide a sense of priorities and a basis for cooperative action within states. The Council of State Historical Records Coordinators, working in concert with national professional associations and the commission, is a focal point for national cooperation or at least focus on common issues such as electronic records management or professional development.

LEADING ARCHIVAL PROGRAMS: TOWARD AN ACTION AGENDA

What should be done to encourage stronger leadership of archival programs? Several steps would be beneficial:

1. Professional associations need to give more attention to the issue of leadership—at their conferences, in their publications, and through the pronouncements of their presidents, officers, and directors. Associations to a significant degree define the field; part of that responsibility is helping to set an agenda for developing archival leadership.

2. There is a need for better measures of attainment and success for archival programs. How should we measure success? How shall we evaluate the fruits of archival leadership? To what standards should those to whom archival program directors report hold them?

3. We need more and better vehicles for sharing information on archival leadership issues, e.g., websites, listservs, case studies. Questions that might be explored include: How to define archival leadership issues? How is archival leadership similar to, and how is it different from, leadership in other settings? What are the most effective strategic approaches? What approaches were tried that were less than successful, and why?

4. Universities preparing archival managers and leaders of the future need to develop more courses in leadership and more opportunities for students to see leadership-in-action through practice, field studies, and internships.

Archival program leadership requires energy, talent, and dedication. But the rewards are worth the cost in terms of the long-term social benefit of well-administered archival programs.

APPENDIX A: ARCHIVAL LEADERSHIP AND POLITICAL LEADERSHIP

Exemplary leaders of archival programs are in many ways like the best political leaders: they are visionary, energetic, pragmatic, politically savvy, and aspire to greatness for their program. Soon after a new president of the United States takes office, says David Gergen, someone whispers a quiet word in his ear: "Did you know that there is still room up there on Mount Rushmore for one more face? At least a small profile." Actually, there isn't room there, but every president aspires to the greatness of the four men remembered there; every great archival leader aspires to be remembered for stellar program building. Gergen describes seven traits of great presidents; the list is worth looking at as a guide for great archivists. From David Gergen, *Eyewitness to Power: The Essence of Leadership, Nixon to Clinton* (New York: Simon and Schuster, 2000), 343–352.

1. *Leadership starts from within.* "The inner soul of a president flows into every aspect of his leadership. . . . his passions in life usually form the basis for his central mission in office." Physical energy, personal integrity, good judgment, and faith in the future are traits that lead to wise decisions and responsible leadership.

2. *A central, compelling purpose.* A president needs a clear vision and purpose and "must tell the country where he is heading so he can rally people behind him." That central purpose must be rooted in the nation's core values and traditions.

3. *A capacity to persuade.* This trait has obvious insights for archival leaders. It consists mostly of the ability to speak well, to articulate and convey a clear message, to gauge it to the audience, to make it obvious that the message is heartfelt.

4. *An ability to work within the system.* A president needs to see himself as being at the center of a web that includes the public, Congress, the press, domestic interest groups, domestic elites (people with exceptional interest in the government and ability to influence it), and foreign powers. The leader needs to deal with all of these groups, ascertain their needs, and understand how to work with them for the benefit of the program.

5. *A quick, sure start.* "Hit the ground running" is good advice for a new president, and for a new archival program director. There is a need to achieve a smooth, successful start, to make the values clear, and to show a firm hand at directing. Of course, this does not mean that the leader is not open to new ideas or that patient consensus building is not important. It does mean that there is a need for some action and motion from the beginning of one's tenure.

6. *Strong, prudent advisors.* Gergen notes that the best presidents are those who surround themselves with the best advisers. The best archival program directors look for strong deputies and department heads, people who have experience and independent ideas, who sometimes question or challenge the director's vision in a positive, constructive way, and who are similar to the director in their commitment to the program and their willingness to put in extra work for its benefit.

7. *Inspiring others to carry on the mission.* The best presidents "create a living legacy, inspiring legions of followers to carry on their missions long after they are gone." So also, the best archival leaders create a program that is so distinctive, strong, and progressive that it continues to be outstanding long after the leader has departed.

APPENDIX B: ARCHIVAL LEADERSHIP AND BUSINESS LEADERSHIP

Leading an archival program is in many ways similar to leading a dynamic, successful business. The key to success in business these days seems to be leadership that encourages and fosters change, reading customer needs and changing to anticipate how they are going to change, expanding into unserved or underserved areas, and really listening to people in your own organization who advocate innovations based on their own insights and perceptions of how the field is changing. "Never has incumbency been worth less," warns Gary Hamel. Old business models are changing, old companies are innovating, new companies are rising up on good ideas, and leaders are imagining the future and then creating it. Developing innovation requires challenging old management tenets, he argues. Rebuild or build anew, he advises, by discarding old bricks and putting in new ones; his list, below, should suggest some approaches for archives. Quoted from Gary Hamel, *Leading the Revolution* (Boston: Harvard Business School Press, 2000), 280–281.

Old Brick	New Brick
Top management is responsible for setting strategy	Everybody can help build innovative strategies
Getting better, faster is the way to win	Rule-busting innovation is the way to win
Information technology creates competitive advantage	Unconventional business concepts create competitive advantage
Being revolutionary is high risk	More of the same is high risk
We can merge our way to competitiveness	There's no correlation between size and profitability
Innovation equals new products and new technologies	Innovation equals entirely new concepts
Strategy is the easy part; implementation is the hard part	Strategy is the easy part only if you're content to be an imitator
Change starts at the top	Change starts with activists
Our real problem is execution	Our real problem is incrementalism
Alignment is always a virtue	Diversity and variety are the keys to innovation
Big companies can't innovate	Big companies can become gray-haired revolutionaries
Incumbents will always lose to entrepreneurial start-ups	You can bring the discipline of Silicon Valley inside
You can't make innovation a capability	Oh yes you can, but not without effort

NOTES

1. Society of American Archivists, "Introduction," in *The Society of American Archivists: Description and Brief History, http://www.archivists.org/history.html.*

2. Most of the strategic planning reports issued by the various State Historical Records Advisory Boards in the 1990's provide documentation of the mismatch between level of needs vs. levels of resources and of the need for better planning, clearer priorities, and stronger leadership. See for instance NYS Historical Records Advisory Board, *Ensuring a Future for Our Past* (Albany: NYS Historical Records Advisory Board, 1997), South Carolina State Historical Records Advisory Board, *Into the 21st Century: A Plan for South Carolina's Historical Records, 2000–2005* (Columbia: SC State Historical Records Advisory Board, 2000), and Council of State Historical Records Coordinators, *Where History Begins: A Report on Historical Records Repositories in the United States* (Washington: The Council, 1998).

3. Warren Bennis, *On Becoming a Leader* (Reading, MA: Addison-Wesley, 1989), 45.

4. Martin W. Sandler and Deborah A. Hudson, *Beyond the Bottom Line: How to Do More with Less in Nonprofit and Public Organizations* (New York: Oxford University Press, 1998), 10.

5. Max DePree, *Leadership Is an Art* (New York: Doubleday, 1989), 9–19.

6. See Bruce W. Dearstyne, *Managing Historical Records Programs* (New York: Alta Mira Press and American Association for State and Local History, 2000), 27–30.

7. Burt Nanus, *Visionary Leadership: Creating a Compelling Sense of Direction in Your Organization* (San Francisco: Jossey-Bass, 1992), 3, 4.

8. Rosabeth Moss Kanter, "The Enduring Skills of Change Leaders," *Leader to Leader* 13 (Summer 1999), Drucker Foundation for Not-for-Profit Management, *http://www.pfdf.org/leaderbooks/L2L/summer99/kanter.html.*

9. John P. Kotter, *Leading Change* (Boston: Harvard Business School Press, 1996), 3–16.

10. William E. Fulmer, *Shaping the Adaptive Organization: Landscapes, Learning, and Leadership in Volatile Times* (New York: AMACOM, 2000), 152–173.

11. Rosabeth Moss Kanter, "Restoring People to the Heart of the Organization of the Future," in Frances Hesselbein et al. eds., *The Organization of the Future* (New York: Drucker Foundation, 1997), 139–150.

12. Quoted from Marcus Buckingham and Curt Coffman, *First, Break All the Rules: What the World's Greatest Managers Do Differently* (New York: Simon and Schuster, 1999), 28.

13. James M. Kouzes and Barry Z. Posner, *Encouraging the Heart: A Leader's Guide to Rewarding and Recognizing Others* (San Francisco: Jossey-Bass, 1999), 3–14.

14. Anne J. Gilliland-Swetland, *Enduring Paradigm, New Opportunities: The Value of the Archival Perspective in the Digital Environment* (Washington: Council on Library and Information Resources, 2000), 1.

15. Peter Drucker, *Managing the Non-Profit Organization: Practices and Principles* (New York: Harper Business, 1992), 18–19, 201.

9

Building Strong Archival Programs: Insights and Approaches

Bruce W. Dearstyne

This concluding chapter of the book presents some concrete examples of perceptive insights and progressive practices. Several themes run through these material presented here: inclination to change in response to changing times, continual revisiting and refreshing of program vision and mission, commitment to dynamic program building, strategic approach to the work, planning as a program building device, and building alliances and networks. Each of the examples represents promising examples of genuine *archival leadership*.

LEADERSHIP QUALIFICATIONS FOR ARCHIVAL PROGRAM DIRECTORS

The most successful programs have dynamic, well-qualified program directors who bring to their positions a combination of the power of envisioning, the knack of strategizing, the ability to inspire, and the personal energy to persevere, even in the face of hardships and setbacks. Institutions need to recognize the complexity of administering an archival program that may be misunderstood as being a relatively simple operation. In reality, archival programs are complex and a high level of leadership is required. Institutions need to set the stage by recruiting and hiring as directors people who, through a combination of education, experience, and personal style, are well suited to leading the program. The following statement is a good example of the set of skills that are needed.

STATEMENT OF PREFERRED QUALIFICATIONS FOR DIRECTORS OF LARGE-SCALE GOVERNMENT RECORDS AND ARCHIVAL PROGRAMS[1]

Records and Archives Programs: Essential to Sound, Effective Government.

NAGARA, the national professional association that is dedicated to the improvement of federal, state, and local government records and information management, believes that the importance of government records and archival programs necessitates the appointment of highly effective leaders and administrators to direct these programs.

Records and archives programs are essential to the sound, effective, responsive operation of government. Government at all levels is changing and adapting to meet shifting public expectations, service needs, resources levels, and changes in our economy and society. Its records and information resources are essential to the sound management of government itself, to the delivery of services, and to the documentation of its work. Records represent a major investment of time and governmental resources. The widespread use of computers, telecommunications technology, and the dramatic shift to the creation and use of electronic records and information present records management problems of unprecedented magnitude and complexity. Managing government records and information today is a demanding challenge that requires skill, dedication, understanding of management techniques, and a capacity to adopt new techniques to meet changing issues and needs.

Leadership and Administrative Abilities of Program Directors

The programs charged with the sound administration of records, with providing advisory services to government offices, and with ensuring the continuing availability of records with enduring value, must be led and administered by well-qualified, experienced, dedicated people. Program directors must be able to deal with complex, rapidly changing issues; operate effectively within their program's administrative setting in the government; deal effectively with an array of resource allocators, customers, and others who have an interest or stake in their programs; make optimal use of available financial and other resources; and carry out oversight and supervisory responsibilities. People being considered for program directors' positions should exhibit the ability to:

- Understand the nature of records and their importance in supporting and documenting the government's business and in promoting open government.
- Provide leadership, including setting direction, defining the program's mission and vision, securing support from the government, customers,

and the program's employees, and keeping the program dynamic in meeting changing conditions and needs.

- Build alliances within and beyond government, focusing on areas where there is a strategic advantage in cooperating or partnering with other agencies or groups.

- Act as an effective advocate, spokesperson, and communicator for the program.

- Foster a work environment where employees' morale and productivity are high.

- Ensure the delivery of the highest quality work which is responsive to customer needs.

- Manage on a day-to-day basis, including developing and carrying out workplans and budgets, making the best use of available resources, organizing work, and monitoring and supervising staff.

- Evaluate and report on the program's work.

Preferred Qualifications

Candidates for administrative positions should be able to demonstrate, through a combination of education and experience, that they can carry out the responsibilities noted above in an effective, professional manner. The makeup of the education and experience will vary with the particular position. Whenever possible appointing authorities should seek candidates who have *both* a very strong educational background *and* extensive, progressively responsible experience. In some cases, extensive experience in a particular area might compensate for modest educational preparation, and *vice versa*.

Candidates should be widely recruited and evaluated solely with regard to their professional qualifications and potential to successfully administer the programs which will become their responsibilities.

With the information noted above as a framework, NAGARA recommends the following educational and experiential qualifications:

Education. NAGARA recommends that candidates for directors' positions possess at least a masters' degree in library or information science, history, public administration, or a closely related field. Preference should be given to qualified applicants who have taken extensive graduate courses or specialized in archives or records management. Short of that, substantial course work or workshops or seminars in archives, records management, or closely related information management fields should be regarded as highly desirable. Additional professional qualifications, e.g., certified archivist or certified records manager, are also desirable.

Experience. Candidates should be able to demonstrate that they have experience and ability in the areas noted above. This will usually require at least four years' of leadership, administrative, or supervisory experience. The experience should have been in a setting and circumstances that occasioned the development and application of the abilities outlined above. It is highly desirable that the experience have been in an archives, records, or related information program, e.g., in such areas as: developing records or archives program policies; developing and implementing workplans and budgets; supervising staff; evaluating and reporting on programs; or administering an element of a records or archival program, e.g., appraisal, reference, or public programming.

FOSTERING DEVELOPMENT OF NEW COMPETENCIES FOR ARCHICAL PROFESSIONALS

Successful programs depend on the knowledge, skills, and abilities of their professional staff members. Increasingly, archival professionals need to be proficient not only in archival principles and precepts but also in a broader range of analytical, communication, negotiating, and management skills. They need to carry out their work in a context of change and complexity, to stay flexible and open to change, and to blend traditional practices with new and emerging approaches. *Improvization* is an important trait to develop. Those broader skills—in the business/management, interpersonal, and personal areas—are summarized below.

COMPETENCY PROFILE: INFORMATION RESOURCE MANAGEMENT SPECIALISTS IN ARCHIVES, LIBRARIES AND RECORDS MANAGEMENT (N.P., 1999), SECTIONS H AND I.[2]

H. Demonstrate Business/Management Skills

Skills	Sub-Skills
1. Demonstrate strategic thinking	1.1 Identify issues and opportunities for one's own organization 1.2 Recommend changes and/or new services
2. Demonstrate planning skills	2.1 Establish priorities 2.2 Define objectives 2.3 Identify required resources 2.4 Prepare action plan
3. Demonstrate financial management skills	3.1 Prepare a budget 3.2 Monitor expenses and revenues
4. Demonstrate organizational skills	4.1 Obtain human, physical, material, and technological resources 4.2 Assign/communicate individual mandates

5. Demonstrate people management skills	5.1	Inspire and motivate colleagues and other contributors
	5.2	Monitor and evaluate team and individual performance
	5.3	Demonstrate coaching skills
	5.4	Demonstrate delegation skills
6. Demonstrate problem-solving skills	6.1	Identify and diagnose the problem
	6.2	Identify possible solutions
	6.3	Select solution
	6.4	Develop and implement solution
7. Demonstrate decision-making skills	7.1	Make timely decisions
	7.2	Make appropriate decisions
8. Demonstrate project management skills	8.1	Create a proposal
	8.2	Develop/implement project plan
	8.3	Monitor project progress
	8.4	Evaluate project

I. Demonstrate Interpersonal Skills

Skills	Sub-Skills	
1. Manage customer expectations	1.1	Respond to client/customer/user needs and expectations
	1.2	Maintain/improve quality of services
	1.3	Easily establish contact with clients/customers/users
	1.4	Maintain long lasting relationships with clients/customers/users
2. Demonstrate oral communication skills	2.1	Give clear directions/instructions
	2.2	Explain complex issues/material in plain language
	2.3	Make various types of formal presentations
3. Demonstrate written communication skills	3.1	Write clearly and concisely
	3.2	Edit documentation
	3.3	Organize complex information to facilitate understanding

4. Demonstrate leadership	4.1 Demonstrate a capacity to influence 4.2 Orient individual and team efforts
5. Demonstrate negotiation skills	5.1 Create a positive climate 5.2 Persuade/argue 5.3 Find a win-win arrangement/settlement
6. Demonstrate interviewing skills	6.1 Create a positive climate 6.2 Use interviewing techniques
7. Demonstrate teamwork skills	7.1 Promote collaboraton/cooperation and share one's experience and expertise 7.2 Earn colleagues' trust and support 7.3 Suggest ideas and adopt behaviors to optimize teamwork

REDEFINING ARCHIVISTS AS INFORMATION MANAGEMENT PROFESSIONALS

Archivists and other information professionals face a continuing challenging of redefining their role in the "information age." That should be an easy assignment; in a sense, we are in the "information business" and now much of the economy, government, and education is dependent on digital information to function. But it is not an easy challenge; it requires considerable imagination, an ability to interpret and explain archival work in terms that technical experts and policy makers can understand, and an ability to make the business case for archival work. Archivists need to maintain their distinctiveness as a profession at the same time that they make clear their role as information professionals. The following statement, prepared for an informal alliance of professional associations, attempts to articulate new approaches.

INFORMATION PROFESSIONALS IN THE DIGITAL ERA[3]

Information's New Importance

During the past few years, *information*, particularly information in electronic or digital form, has assumed a new, central importance in our society, government, business, and education. Information is now recognized as a key strategic resource, the basis for doing business and delivering services, and a sustaining force in economic prosperity. Government and businesses have developed or are developing policies specifically intended to help them guide and manage the use of information. Discussions of how to expand e-commerce, e-business, and e-government are now commonplace.

The Need for Professionals

Information is sometimes equated with *information technology*, a term which refers generally to the use of computers and telecommunications devices and networks to create, transport, and make information available. Actually, the significance and challenges far transcend technology. Information, to be useful and to meet the expectations that our society puts upon it, requires active, focused, sustained attention and management by professionals who are well versed not only in the technology but also in other aspects of information management. Professional attention is needed to help address these issues:

- The traditional, format-based definitions of information resources are being undermined and the distinctions among them are dissolving, e.g., there are no longer hard-and-fast distinctions among formerly clear categories such as "books," "records," "documents," and "databases."

- There is so much information available that simply locating what is needed among a myriad of institutional databases, other internal sources, the World Wide Web, libraries, and other sources, constitutes a daunting challenge.

- Electronic information by its very abundance and omnipresence tends to discourage attention to issues of authenticity, quality, value, and longevity.

- Institutions find it difficult to understand or significantly underestimate the level of technical, human, and other investments needed for optimal information management.

- Companies and other institutions are blindsided in legal actions because they cannot locate needed information or, by contrast, their opponents discover detrimental information assumed to have been destroyed but actually still existing in the company's own e-mail, databases, or other records systems.

- Individual employees find it difficult to understand their own information-related responsibilities, for instance, in saving official records for as long as required by law, regulations, or corporate policies.

- Custodial responsibilities and ownership of information resources are increasingly complicated and unclear.

Principles of Information Management in Institutional Settings

The abundance and importance of information make it necessary to develop and adhere to principles for its management. In the final analysis, development of and fostering adherence to such principles is the work of information professionals.

These principles will of course vary from institution to institution but may include some or all of the following:

- The institution has a carefully-developed, written information policy that provides overall guidance on the strategic creation, management, and use of information.
- The CEO ensures that an individual or office is designated to lead, coordinate, or monitor the implementation of the policy.
- Information and records-related responsibilities of employees are clear.
- The institution has up-to-date computer equipment, software, etc., and makes provision for upgrading and updating as needed.
- There is enterprise-wide provision for continuing education and updating and upgrading of skills so that employees can understand and take advantage of advances in information technology.
- Legal information-related requirements are met, e.g., retention of official records in line with laws regulations or retention schedules.
- Ethical issues, e.g., safeguarding of sensitive or confidential information, are addressed.
- Archival records with historically significant information of the organization are preserved.

The Role of Information Professionals

Information professionals, e.g., librarians, records managers, archivists, municipal clerks, forms managers, and others, play a significant role in guiding the use of information resources. Professions are characterized by such traits as education credentials, a solid body of theoretical and practical knowledge, service orientation and dedication, relative autonomy and independence in work, independent judgment, ability to meet complex issues, and adherence to a code of ethics. In the complicated digital information environment of today, information professionals play some or all of these roles:

- Intermediaries among people, information, and technology.
- Clarifiers whose professional training and continually updated skills enable them to understand the nature of information, the relationship among various types of information, the role of computers and other devices in the creation and management of digital information, and the strategic role of information.
- Custodians of important information resources such as records, archives, and books in the corporate library.
- Access experts who understand the makeup and value of information can assist in formulating inquiries, and can help people get at the information they need when they need it.
- Educators who can provide guidance and help people understand the nature of information resources and how to get at and use them.

- Legal experts who can develop policies to ensure compliance with legal information creation, maintenance, and disclosure requirements and help ensure that the institution is on firm ground in case of litigation that requires access to records and other information.

- Program and financial advisors who can provide advice on the purchase of information-related equipment and services.

- Honest brokers who can objectively mediate among genuinely competing interests, e.g., over the degree of access to information.

- Reporters who can measure the cost of information creation and management and the cost savings and avoidance associated with optimal information use and who can explain and report on it in terms that non-experts can readily understand.

Associations of Information Professionals

Professional associations are a sustaining force in this rapidly-changing field. Professional associations:

- Provide standards and guidelines for educational programs and certification programs for individuals to ensure that professionals have the knowledge, skills, and abilities needed to carry out their work in a consistent, satisfactory manner.

- Issue technical standards and other publications that establish guidelines for sound information management.

- Define and clarify issues that need policy attention, e.g, by state or federal government, and bring them to the attention of appropriate parties through advocacy work.

- Through their conferences, provide forums for professionals to meet, exchange views, learn from each other, and generally to build on each others' experience in an arena where experiential learning is essential to cope with complex, constantly evolving problems.

- Promulgate ethical standards to guide professional conduct.

- Collaborate with each other, e.g., through the Collaborative of Information Management Associations.

EXPLAINING THE ARCHIVES' VISION AND MISSION

The most successful programs have been able to define, or redefine, their vision and mission in terms that fit their programs, are appropriate for the times, and are meaningful to the executives in the parent institution whose support and resources are critical. Archives are important for history and heritage, but they need to be operated in a businesslike fashion and to communicate that intention. At the same time, their mission and vision statements need a quality of *eloquence*. One of the best examples of creative reinvention, the National Archives and Records Administration, has redefined itself away from the common notion of archives as a repository for old documents and asserts instead that it is a forward-looking institution that effectively serves the government and the people.

READY ACCESS TO ESSENTIAL EVIDENCE: THE STRATEGIC PLAN OF THE NATIONAL ARCHIVES AND RECORDS ADMINISTRATION, 1997–2007, "STRATEGIC DIRECTIONS FOR THE NATIONAL ARCHIVES AND RECORDS ADMINISTRATION"[4]

Vision

NARA

The National Archives is a public trust on which our democracy depends. It enables people to inspect for themselves the record of what government has done. It enables officials and agencies to review their actions and helps citizens hold them accountable. It ensures continuing access to essential evidence that documents:

> the rights of American citizens,
> the actions of Federal officials, and
> the national experience.

To be effective, we at NARA must determine what evidence is essential for such documentation, ensure that government creates such evidence, and make it easy for users to access that evidence regardless of where it is, or where they are, for as long as needed. We also must find technologies, techniques, and partners world-wide that can help improve service and hold down costs, and we must help staff members continuously expand their capability to make the changes necessary to realize the vision.

Mission

NARA ensures for the citizen and the public servant, for the president and the congress and the courts, ready access to essential evidence.

Goals

One: Essential evidence will be created, identified, appropriately scheduled, and managed for as long as needed.

Two: Essential evidence will be easy to access regardless of where it is or where users are for as long as needed.

Three: All records will be preserved in appropriate space for use as long as needed.

Four: NARA's capabilities for making the changes necessary to realize our vision will continuously expand.

Values

To succeed in our mission, all of us within NARA need to value the following:

Risk-taking: experiment, take chances, try new ways, learn from mistakes, be open to change

Communication: propose ideas, dialogue with others, develop trust, and act openly, honestly, and with integrity

Commitment: be responsible, accountable, and always willing to learn

Loyalty: support the mission, help fellow workers, proceed as a team, and recognize that our government and our people truly need our service.

DEMONSTRATING THE USEFULNESS OF ARCHIVES

The most impressive archival programs have a knack for demonstrating the importance of what they do and of conveying it to a variety of audiences using imaginative examples. The most telling examples are ones that show in dramatic terms how archives affect the destinies of institutions and how they change people's lives. The following is a good example of demonstrating usefulness in personal terms.

WHAT WOULD YOU DO? [5]

A homeowner wonders about a marshy area in back of his property. It might have been a wetland at some point, but appears to have been filled in. When was this done? Was clean fill used? Did the town sanction it? He doesn't know where to begin looking for records or whether, if any exist, he would be permitted to see them.

The public library has a unique collection of eighteenth-century maps showing the wetland area. The purchase of the land and construction of the house is well documented in a collection of family papers at the local historical society. At the town hall, selectmen minutes from the turn of the century reveal that the wetland was used as a dumping ground for a tannery. All these records are public and accessible- but unknown to the homeowner.

The man was adopted. He never really wondered about his biological parents until now. Getting on in years, he has developed severe heart problems. How much of this is related to his genetic background? Could this affect his children and grandchildren? Are they at higher risk? Should they take precautions?

A case file containing his mother's medical history was destroyed when the adoption agency went out of business. Records stayed in a basement for a number of years until they were damaged by a flood, became moldy, and were discarded as useless. The man will never find the information he seeks.

The quality of a critical component of the nuclear power plant is in question. The original computer-aided designs have been revised and overwritten; no original

designs for the equipment in the plant can be found. How can the manufacturer and
the plant owner make informed decisions about the safety of the equipment?

> Without the information policies and retention schedules in place to ensure
> the creation, management, and preservation of long-term records, businesses
> cannot fulfill their legal obligations; workers and public health could be at
> risk.

A researcher is trying to discover the history of a nineteenth-century African
American community in a Massachusetts city. She searches the holdings of local libraries, historical societies, and other repositories, but can find no trace of the people who lived in the neighborhood for nearly one hundred years.

> Despite the fact that minority groups make up a growing 20 percent of the
> Massachusetts population, only a tiny fraction of repositories actively collect
> records relating to minority communities and culture; an even smaller frac-
> tion report significant holdings in these areas. Because no mechanisms exist
> to identify gaps in the documentary record, it is difficult for repositories to es-
> tablish collaborative strategies for collecting records. Some creators who hold
> important records would be interested in depositing records— if repositories
> approached them.

MAKING THE CASE FOR SUPPORT FOR ARCHIVAL PROGRAMS

The most effective archival leaders have a knack for identifying themes,
turning a phrase, striking the right note, and tailoring their message to their
audience. The best messages connect, engage, challenge, and point the way
toward better appreciation and use of archives. They make the case that institutions and governments have a responsibility for archival records. This
example is from a document intended for governmental leadership and the
general public in New York State.

A CHALLENGE FOR THE PEOPLE AND ORGANIZATIONS OF NEW YORK [6]

New Yorkers value their heritage.
New Yorkers neglect their heritage.

Each of the above statements is true—and therein lies the challenge.
Diaries of a farm woman, account books from a hardware store, minutes of a local zoning board, an oral interview with a traditional Mohawk basket maker, photos of a Puerto Rican baseball team, and the membership rolls of a Black Baptist
church—these are some of the ways New Yorkers preserve their history, their culture, and their collective memory. Together they are an incomparable resource for
students and teachers, for the business community, for journalists, for folklorists,
for documentary film makers, for genealogists, for government officials, and for all
New Yorkers. More than 2,500 historical societies, libraries, archives, museums, and
other organizations in New York State have endeavored to preserve this heritage ...

Yet many serious issues remain to be addressed. There are significant gaps in our historical documentation, leaving important industries, events, people, cultures, and organizations virtually undocumented, and therefore unknowable for the future. Most of the institutions preserving historical records are seriously understaffed, undertrained and underfunded. Existing historical records are too often inaccessible to potential users. A public that thrills to Ken Burns' Civil War documentary, that attends heritage festivals to celebrate its cultural identity, and whose members in droves trace their family roots is a public in active pursuit of its history. Yet that public is being denied important opportunities and resources because of the inadequate condition of New York's documentary heritage.

FOSTERING ARCHIVAL COOPERATION

One of the challenges to archival program leadership is to identify ways of cooperating on issues of common concern. This approach permits a pooling of resources and talent, provides an opportunity for programs to draw on each other's expertise, fosters solutions to difficult problems, and generally helps advance the archival enterprise. The most promising strategic approaches are the various statewide plans prepared by the State Historical Records Advisory Boards in the various states that seek to build the capacity of archival programs to meet their obligations. The directors of state archival programs, who also serve as State Historical Records Coordinators and chair the boards, exercise leadership skills in carrying out analyses of statewide issues and developing strategic plans that foster cooperation. One of the best is South Carolina's, which sets a clear agenda for statewide action over the next few years. An excerpt is provided here:

THE STATE PLAN: ELEMENTS AND PERFORMANCE [7]

Priority A: Educate the public on the importance of historical records

Goal: Increase public awareness, support, and understanding of archives and records management

Objective 1: Cultivate understanding of the significance of historical records among those who use and create them

Objective 2: Increase awareness of archival and records management programs

Objective 3: Promote coalition building in support of historical records programs

Priority B: Increase financial support for South Carolina's historical records

Goal: Seek the resources necessary to address the needs of historical records

Objective 1: Pursue the financial resources that enable the SC SHRAB to continue as a granting agency

Objective 2: Increase the number of grant proposals from South Carolina Institutions

Priority C: Increase archival education/training and program development

Goal: Enhance the knowledge and skill of those who work with historical records

Objective 1: Promote and support educational and training opportunities for those with historical records responsibilities

Objective 2: Improve coordination of and collaboration among outreach and training programs offered by professional associations, universities, and the SCDAH

Priority D: Ensure the preservation and accessibility of South Carolina's historical records

Goal I: Improve the documentation of South Carolina History, especially regarding underdocumented subjects and social groups

Objective 1: Identify the significant gaps in historical documentation of the state's history

Objective 2: Support and encourage the collection, preservation, and use of historical records for under-documented groups, organizations, and communities

Goal II: Improve the public knowledge of and access to South Carolina's historical records

Objective 1: Make the availability of historical records more widely known

Objective 2: Encourage use of nationally-recognized standards to provide wider access to historical records

Goal III: Improve the preservation of historical records

Objective 1: Promote the use of nationally-recognized standards for the care, maintenance, and preservation of collections

Objective 2: Encourage collaborative projects to improve the preservation of historical records

Objective 3: Foster educational opportunities to improve preservation knowledge and skills

Goal IV: Promote the establishment and/or improvement of records management programs

Objective 1: Identify needs, establish priorities, and develop strategies for records management programs

Objective 2: Support and promote the establishment of a local records management improvement fund

Priority E: Address the challenges posed by the proliferation of information technology and electronic records

Goal: Encourage and promote the effective management of historical records

Objective 1: Promote educational opportunities for those who are responsible for creating, identifying, managing, and using historical records

Objective 2: Encourage information-sharing on standards and best practices for managing historical records

Objective 3: Promote public awareness of the problems in managing electronic records over time

Priority F: Ensure a productive and visible State Historical Records Advisory Board

Goal I : Secure staff support adequate for the work of the board and the achievement of the goals and objectives of the state plan

Goal II: Continue the board's role in strategic planning

Objective 1: Monitor and report progress on the state plan goals and objectives

Objective 2: Annually review the plan and adjust as circumstances warrant

Goal III: Collaborate with other organizations and institutions in support of historical records

Objective 1: Promote information-sharing, cooperation, and concerted action

Objective 2: Encourage programs and projects that address key elements of the state plan

STAKING OUT NEW POSITIONS ON ELECTRONIC ARCHIVAL RECORDS

Managing electronic archival records is probably the single greatest challenge faced by the leaders of major archival programs today. This challenge has occasioned new approaches to archival work, including some that are substantially different from the past. The National Archives of Australia has developed a very impressive set of planning documents and guidelines that redefine its role and advocate a partnership between the Archives and its customers, the government agencies it serves. This new approach includes asking the agencies themselves to maintain custody of archival records rather than transferring them to the archives. The document below summarizes this new approach.

MANAGING ELECTRONIC RECORDS: THE STRATEGY[8]

The Agency's Role

The best prospect for maintaining electronic records and ensuring their accessibility over time is for such records to remain with the agencies which create or manage them. This strategy ensures that the essential characteristics of records are maintained. For instance, individual agencies are most likely to understand their electronic systems and the specific applications required to maintain the records they contain. Furthermore, the strategy also ensures that electronic records remain accessible. As technology changes over time, agencies are best placed to ensure that records of enduring value are successfully transferred or migrated as systems evolve.

The success of this approach requires identification and timely disposal of records with limited administrative value and the preservation of access to those records which have continuing administrative values. Efficient and accountable recordkeeping systems rely on strategic planning and management control. Unplanned and uncontrolled recordkeeping systems and accumulations of records are a danger to sound administration and cost the administration and ultimately the community.

The Archives' Role

While the archives is in a position to manage some electronic records, it does not have the technology or resources to manage electronic records from all the electronic systems and applications currently in place in the Commonwealth. Even if resources were available to take on such a role it would entail the archives becoming a museum of obsolete technology—not a sensible option in the face of rapid technological change and an ultimate exercise in futility. As a consequence the archives will accept custody of electronic records in circumstances where we have the technology and resources to do so.

These cases are where:

The agency which created the electronic records is about to be or has become defunct and no agency is identifiable as its successor to the function.

The archives enters into an agreement with an agency to take custody of the electronic records.

Where the archives has agreed to accept custody of electronic records from an agency, the archives and the agency need to ensure that the records are transferred to the archives appropriately; that is, accompanied by the information and metadata necessary for maintaining access to the records.

The success of the strategy will, of course, depend on close cooperation and support between the archives and individual agencies. For our part, we have developed policy guidance standards to help you manage electronic records such as *Keeping Electronic Records* and *Managing Electronic Messages as Records*. We are in the process of developing guidelines on the legal admissibility of electronic records and desktop management. In addition, the Archives can assist you in the following ways:

Work with you to identify the electronic records in your custody which are of enduring value and as such need to be maintained and made accessible over time in order to meet administrative and/or archival requirements.

Work with you to identify and dispose of the electronic records in your custody which are not of enduring value.

Assist you in identifying the information or metadata which needs to be captured and maintained with electronic records of enduring value if they are to remain identifiable and accessible over time.

Provide advice on access to archival electronic records so that you can meet the access provisions of the Archives Act-and take advantage of its safeguard provisions.

Assist you with the development of recordkeeping systems through the provision of appropriate advice on when and how records need to be created.

Working Together

In short, we will work with you to ensure that your electronic record system is manageable by helping you consolidate your electronic records and by helping you identify appropriate maintenance procedures. In addition, we can help you determine the length of time different types of electronic records should be kept. Our aim is to ensure that you are not using your resources to maintain ephemera or to manage records which are no longer needed. In general, then, electronic records will remain in the custody of the agencies which create and manage them. Maintaining records, however, is a shared responsibility. The Archives will work with you to ensure that you can manage and maintain the electronic records in your custody efficiently and effectively.

JOINING BROADER INFORMATION MANAGEMENT INITIATIVES

One of the most promising strategies being pursued by the best led archival programs is to ally themselves with, and contribute to, broader information management initiatives in their institutions. This strategy provides visibility and influence for the program and, at the same time, gives it leverage to help ensure that electronic records issues are addressed in the planning and development of large scale information systems. One of the best examples is the Minnesota State Archives in the Minnesota Historical Society. Going well beyond traditional archival functions, this program has developed guidance on "Trustworthy Information Systems" which ties sound archival and records management practices to broader information practices which benefit its parent agency (state government), ensure systematic documentation, and help manage the information resources needed for legal actions. The section below introduces and explains the importance of a trustworthy system.

WHAT IS A TRUSTWORTHY INFORMATION SYSTEM? [9]

Trustworthiness refers to an information system's accountability and its ability to produce reliable and authentic information and records. We chose the term trustworthy because it denotes integrity, ability, faith, and confidence. We use trustworthiness to describe information system accountability. We use the words reliable and authentic when we talk about the information and records that the information system creates. Reliability indicates a record's authority and is established when a record is created. Authenticity ensures that a record will be reliable throughout its life, whether that lifetime lasts six months, ten years, twenty years, or forever.

Government creates a lot of information and records, in a variety of ways and formats, and for a number of reasons. The most obvious reason that we create records is simply to do our business, whether that business means running the governor's office, managing the state's welfare system, or keeping track of spending for a county, city, school district, or township.

There's another reason for creating records: government accountability. Information and records generated in the course of government business must reflect government's accountability. Government reports and is accountable to its "bosses," that is, elected officials, and ultimately, the citizens who voted for them. Government records document and provide evidence that government is going about its business wisely or unwisely. They indicate whether government business gets managed and conducted properly in accordance with laws, statutes, regulations, and other requirements. Government records also document the history of our state; they contain valuable information about Minnesota's citizens and the social, economic, political, and natural environments in which we live.

Government accountability needs to be considered as information systems are developed. Computer-based information systems can do any number of tasks quickly and efficiently, but we don't always know who is accountable for these systems and the information that they create. The computer, unlike a human being, does not bear accountability for itself; people in government make information systems accountable. It follows, then, that in building information systems, we need to establish and create procedures, system documentation, and descriptions of system information as a means to make the system accountable.

We need trustworthy information systems to ensure our accountability as government agencies.

COLLECTIVELY ADDRESSING THE CHALLENGES OF ELECTRONIC RECORDS

The challenge of electronic archival records is one of several the profession faces where we need strong leadership and decisive, collective action. Individual programs acting alone, even if they take novel approaches as Australia is doing, are unlikely to meet this immense challenge. We need to reconceptualize what is meant by a record in an electronic setting; to develop effective tools to deal with these records; to update our expertise; and to position our programs at the intersection of records, information technology, and information policy. Research in this area needs to shift from a narrow focus on records systems to a broader view that places records in the context of institutional information management. One proposed agenda that takes that forward-looking approach is reproduced below.

RESEARCH AND DEVELOPMENT FRAMEWORK FOR RECORDS AND INFORMATION MANAGEMENT[10]

The Need for a Research and Development Framework

The ARMA Educational Foundation has developed a Research and Development Framework to help focus and provide context, direction, and priorities for research and development efforts in records and information management. This field is undergoing change of unprecedented magnitude and velocity due to the rapid restructuring of governments and other institutions; the impact of computers, digital technology, the Internet, and the World Wide Web; and changing needs and expectations on the part of customers of information as to how they seek and use information. The changes in the field wrought by technology and other forces have made many traditional approaches obsolete, occasioned a substantial revision of others, and brought the need to develop substantially new policies and programs that are suited to the new information management challenges.

Information managers need and are asking for fresh thinking, new perspectives, and new products and tools to deal with the challenges their programs face, particularly in dealing with the impact and implications of information technology. However, technology changes have come about so fast that there has not been time for either enough thoughtful analysis or research and development efforts to fully generate the new approaches and products that are needed. To date, technology and institutional change have outdistanced information programs' capacities to accommodate and deal with them, in part because research and development efforts have been less than adequate. There has not been a consensus on the questions or areas most in need of attention. There has been a scattering of efforts, which has resulted in less than optimal use of very limited time, limited funding, and other research/development resources. Projects are too often carried out in isolation, out of communication with other project leaders, and without a framework to indicate priority categories where the work is most needed and most critical. Much of the research that has been done, including some that has produced excellent products, has had limited impact because its results have not been made known or tested in actual records and information management settings.

The Foundation's Aims

The Foundation, a newly organized entity that supports research and education, believes there is a need for a clearer sense of what should be accomplished in research and development if our field is to master its challenges and continue its long record of service to individuals, institutions, and society. The Foundation hopes to lead, coordinate, foster, and facilitate focused research and development efforts. We envision our main role, particularly in the next few years, to be a catalytic one of fostering, coordinating, and providing encouragement to others and, where appropriate, working in partnership with them. In the future, as resources are available, we hope to provide direct funding for focused research and development efforts. We expect to seek funds for the Foundation's educational and research sponsorship work and hope to carry out other initiatives such as symposia and educational forums to review the status of research/development efforts and keep up with changes in the field. . . .

The emphasis of research and development initiatives should be in areas where information professionals need new strategies, products, and tools right away to deal with the implications of information technology and other issues. Initiatives need to focus on research *and development* to address critical issues in a timely, effective fashion. The approach should be pragmatic: identify a problem or issue, review best practices, look at actual records and information settings, carry out analysis, develop solutions or recommendations, bring a report or other product to completion in a timely fashion, and widely disseminate the results. The field, propelled by technology, is moving too fast, and the needs are too great, for long, drawn-out projects.

Initial List of Research and Development Areas

The following is an initial list of proposed priority areas for research and development initiatives. The list is not in priority order.

- How to survey, monitor, measure, and track changes in recordkeeping needs and practices in modern offices, particularly in an electronic setting.

- How to reconceptualize what constitutes a "record" in an electronic setting and state it in a concrete, understandable way, e.g., in a statutory definition in government or in regulations or directives for businesses

- How to further develop and apply the concepts of "recordkeeping system" and "corporate memory" in institutional settings.

- How to tie information management issues and concerns to the notion of information as a key strategic resource/asset that drives business, supports services, etc.

- How to tie records issues and concerns to the development of information policy in government and other institutions.

- How to develop benchmarks and measurements for the technical aspects of this field.

- How to articulate, dramatize, and raise the visibility of records and information management and the work of professionals in this field.

- How to deal with the records implications of home pages and websites, including their use to access records and their records management implications.

- How to build effective partnerships and cooperation among information management professionals who have important influence on records creation and management, e.g., computer specialists, information technology experts, auditors, institutional counsel, program managers.

- How to develop the most effective approaches to education and continuing professional development in this field.

NOTES

1. National Association of Government Archives and Records Administrators, prepared by Bruce Dearstyne, *Statement of Preferred Qualifications for Directors of Large-Scale Government Records and Archival Programs*, January 1999, http://www.nagara.org.

2. Alliance of Libraries, Archives, and Records Management (ALARM), *Competency Profile: Information Resources Management Specialists in Archives, Libraries and Records Management* (n.p., 1999). Reprinted with permission of the Cultural Human Resources Council. This document includes considerable additional detail, including Performance Indicators for each of the sub-skills. It is also presents a description of the more traditional archival knowledge that professionals in this field will need.

3. "Information Professionals in the Digital Era," draft by Bruce Dearstyne for the Collaborative of Information Management Associations, 2000.

4. National Archives and Records Administration, *Ready Access to Essential Evidence: The Strategic Plan of the National Archives and Records Administration, 1997–2007* (Washington: NARA, 2000), 7–8, "What Do We Want to Achieve?"

5. Massachusetts Historical Records Advisory Board, *A Community Treasure: Massachusetts Historical Records—The Summary Plan* (Boston: Massachusetts Historical Records Advisory Board, 1999), *http://www.state.ma.us/sec/arc/arcaac/aacintro/htm*, "What Would You Do?"

6. New York State Historical Records Advisory Board, *Ensuring a Future for Our Past* (Albany: State Historical Records Advisory Board, 1998), 1–7.

7. South Carolina State Historical Records Advisory Board, *Into the 21st Century: A Plan for South Carolina's Historical Records, 2000–2005* (Columbia: SC State Historical Records Advisory Board, 2000), Executive Summary, "The State Plan: Elements and Performance."

8. National Archives of Australia, "Managing Electronic Records: The Strategy," 1997, *http://www.naa.gov.au/recordkeeping/er/manage_er/strategy.html*.

9. Minnesota Historical Society, "What Is a Trustworthy Information System," in *Trustworthy Information Systems Handbook* (St. Paul: Minnesota Historical Society, 2000), Section 3, *http://www.mnhs.org.preserve/records/tis/Section3.html*.

10. ARMA International Educational Foundation *Research and Development Framework for Records and Information Management*, drafted by Bruce Dearstyne (Prairie Village, KS, 1998).

Index

About the Contributors

LAUREN R. BROWN is Curator of Archives and Manuscripts, Collection Management and Special Collections Division, University of Maryland Libraries, a position he has held since 1984. He plans, organizes, and directs the work of the Archives and Manuscripts Department, which includes the University Archives and an extensive collection of literary manuscripts and historical records related to the history of Maryland and the surrounding region. Prior to assuming that position, he was Special Collections Librarian at Rice University. He has held several leadership positions in the Mid-Atlantic Regional Archives Conference and the Society of American Archivists.

FRANK G. BURKE is Professor Emeritus at the University of Maryland College of Information Studies, where he began teaching as an adjunct in 1974 and held a full time faculty position from 1988 until his retirement in 1996. He held positions of responsibility in several programs, including the University of Chicago Special Collections, the Library of Congress Manuscripts Division, and the National Archives. He was Executive Director of the National Historical Publications and Records Commission for fourteen years and was Acting Archivist of the United States for three years. Dr. Burke is a Fellow and former President of the Society of American Archivists. He has written and lectured widely on archival topics since his first article was published in the *American Archivist* in 1967. His book *Research and the Manuscript Tradition* was published in 1997.

RICHARD J. COX is a Professor in the University of Pittsburgh School of Information Sciences where he teaches archives and records management. He is the author of six books and numerous articles on this and related subjects. He was elected a Fellow of the SAA in 1989 and is a former Editor of the *American Archivist*. He presently coedits the *Records & Information Management Report*.

BRUCE W. DEARSTYNE is Professor at the College of Information Studies, University of Maryland. Before assuming that position in 1997 he was, for many years, a program director at the New York State Archives and Records Administration. He is the author of many articles and several books, including *Managing Government Records and Information* (1999) and *Managing Historical Records Programs* (2000).

LIISA FAGERLUND was City Recorder for the City of Portland, Oregon, from 1998 to 2001, where she administered archives, records management, and city council affairs. Prior to assuming that position in 1998, she served as Chief of Archives and Records Management for the United Nations and the World Health Organization in New York and Switzerland. Previous positions included State Archivist of Utah and City Archivist of Portland, Oregon. She is an independent consultant specializing in strategic planning and program development for archives, records management, and electronic records.

LARRY J. HACKMAN was Director of the Harry S Truman Presidential Library and Museum in Independence, Missouri, from 1995 to 2000. He was also president of the Truman Library Institute for National and International Affairs. He was Director of the New York State Archives and Records Administration from 1981 to 1995 and, prior to that, served as the first Director of the Records Program of the National Historical Publications and Records Commission in Washington. Earlier, he was Director of Oral History, Director of Special Programs, and Senior Archivist for Domestic and Political Affairs at the John F. Kennedy Library. Hackman is a Fellow of the Society of American Archivists, served on SAA's Council and Executive Committee, and was a Mellon Fellow at the Modern Archives Institute at the University of Michigan and a Littauer Fellow at the School of Government at Harvard. He has written and lectured widely on archives and public history.

MICHAEL J. KURTZ is Assistant Archivist for the Office of Records Services—Washington, DC. He joined the National Archives and Records Administration in 1974 and has worked in various archival and staff positions in the Office of the Federal Records Centers, the Office of Management and Administration, and the Office of the National Archives. He is also an adjunct professor at the University of Maryland's College of Information Studies where he developed and teaches a course in managing cultural institutions. Dr. Kurtz has authored several publications in the areas of archival management, the American Civil War, and World War II. He is President of the Lutheran Historical Society in Gettysburg, PA, and is the cochair of the Society of American Archivists' Management Roundtable.

PHILIP F. MOONEY has been the Manager of the Archives Department for The Coca Cola Company since 1977 where he is in charge of the archives of one of the nation's foremost companies. A Fellow of the Society of American Archivists, Mooney has served as an instructor in more than fifteen Business Archives Workshops. Among his previous publications are chapters in *Advocating Archives: An Introduction to Public Relations for Archivists* (1994) and *The Records of American Business* (1997).